Jesus Speaks

Alex Telman

Published by Alex Telman, 2024.

JESUS SPEAKS

First edition. October 27, 2024.

ISBN: 979-8230311263

Written by Alex Telman.

Author's Note

Dear Reader,

As you journey through these pages, I invite you to pause and reflect on the profound messages woven throughout this narrative. This work is not just a retelling of ancient events; it is a heartfelt exploration of themes that resonate deeply within the human experience: love, sacrifice, redemption, and the enduring power of faith.

In crafting this book, my intent has been to illuminate the teachings that can guide us through our own lives, inspiring us to act with compassion, to embrace vulnerability, and to seek understanding in a world often marked by division. The lessons shared here transcend time and culture, speaking to the universal truth that love is our greatest gift and our most powerful tool for transformation.

Each chapter serves as a reminder that in our moments of struggle, we have the capacity to choose love over fear, to extend grace over judgment, and to pursue unity over division. The stories of struggle and triumph reflect not only the journey of one individual but the collective journey we all share as members of a larger community.

I hope this book stirs something within you—a desire to embody these teachings, to be a source of light in dark times, and to cultivate a world filled with kindness and understanding. As you turn these pages, may you find encouragement to live out the principles of love and compassion in your daily life, inspiring others to do the same.

Thank you for embarking on this journey with me. Together, let us carry these messages forward, allowing them to shape our lives and the world around us.

With gratitude and hope,

- Alex

Chapter 1: The Burden of Love

As I am led through the streets of Jerusalem, the weight of the cross presses heavily on my shoulders, each splinter digging into my flesh. The weight of the cross bears down on me, not just physically but in every fiber of my being. Each step is heavy, laden with the pain of the world I am about to depart.

The scent of spices from the nearby market lingers in the air, mingling with the dust kicked up by the soldiers' boots. I can hear the distant chatter of merchants, the cries of children playing, and the rustle of robes brushing against skin. It is a reminder of life, vibrant and pulsating, even as I prepare to face death.

The sun hangs low in the sky, casting long shadows across the cobblestones, and the air is thick with the murmur of the crowd. Faces blur together—some filled with curiosity, others with scorn, and a few with sorrow. I can hear their whispers, some mocking, others filled with pity. It is a cacophony of emotions that mirrors the turmoil in my heart.

I see a tapestry of faces, each one telling a different story—each one carrying its own burdens, searching for understanding, for compassion.

A woman stands at the edge of the crowd, her face pale, eyes wide with fear and disbelief. I recognize her; she is the mother of a child I once healed. Her grip tightens on her little one, who clings to her leg, sensing her distress. I want to reach out to her, to comfort her, and reassure her that love will endure beyond this moment. But my voice catches in my throat, and I simply continue walking, feeling the ache of unspoken words.

A figure emerges from the crowd, his face a blend of determination and despair. It's Peter, my steadfast friend. His eyes are filled with tears, and I can sense his inner turmoil, the conflict between loyalty and fear. He's trying to push through the throngs of people, desperate to reach me, but the soldiers hold him back. I wish I could tell him that his faith will carry him through, that this moment, painful as it is, will lead to a greater purpose.

A young boy peeks out from behind his mother's skirts, his innocent eyes wide with curiosity. He looks up at me, untainted by the hate of the crowd. In his gaze, I see hope and the potential for a brighter future. I want to smile at him, to show him that love will always prevail, that he will carry the light of this message forward.

I notice a man with crossed arms and a scowl. He glares at me, his face contorted in disbelief. I recognize him as one who questioned my teachings, who doubted the miracles I performed. I feel a twinge of sadness for him—he has closed himself off from love, trapped in skepticism. I silently pray that one day he may find understanding and open his heart.

A frail, elderly woman stands a little further back, leaning heavily on a cane. Her face is lined with wrinkles that tell stories of a long life filled with struggle. Yet, there's a spark in her eyes—she has seen the miracles, she has felt the love. I see her whispering a prayer, and I feel a connection with her, an understanding that transcends words. In her quiet strength, there is an enduring hope.

A Roman soldier stands watch, his face stern and unyielding. His eyes are hardened, reflecting a life of duty and compliance. I wonder what he thinks as he observes this scene—if he feels any doubt or remorse. I can sense his struggle, the conflict between his role and the humanity he witnesses. I silently wish for him to see beyond the orders he follows, to recognize the love that transcends power.

I catch sight of a woman dressed in mourning clothes, her eyes red from crying. She must have lost someone dear to her, perhaps to violence or illness. Her grief is palpable, and I feel a deep ache in my heart for her suffering. I long to reach out, to let her know that her pain is seen, that even in this darkness, there is a promise of comfort.

A small child, no more than five, sits on his father's shoulders, peering over the crowd. His face is innocent, eyes wide with wonder at the spectacle unfolding before him. For a fleeting moment, I wish to pick him up, to show him the joy of life, to share with him the truth that love conquers all. I see the potential for a future shaped by compassion and hope.

Near the front, I notice a scribe, his face twisted in disdain. He holds a scroll, a reminder of the laws and traditions he clings to. I know he has often challenged me, interpreting my words as a threat to his authority. I feel a mixture of pity and sorrow for him—his rigidity has blinded him to the grace that I offer. I hope that one day he may understand the true essence of the law: love.

As I continue my journey, each face becomes a reflection of the world I have come to know—a world filled with pain, hope, love, and despair. I carry their stories with me, each one a thread in the tapestry of humanity. With each step, I silently pray for them all, hoping that my sacrifice will open their hearts to the boundless love I have always sought to share.

I look at the people and I cannot adequately express and they cannot comprehend the depths of this moment. I wish to reach out, to comfort them, to tell them that even in this pain, love prevails. But I also feel a profound sense of acceptance. This path has been set before me, each step leading to the culmination of my purpose. I recall the moments that have brought me here—the healings, the teachings, the parables that stirred hearts. I am not merely a victim of circumstance; I am fulfilling a promise made long ago, a prophecy that speaks of suffering and redemption.

As the crowd shouts, I feel the weight of their expectations. Some see me as a king, others as a blasphemer. Yet, in this moment, I am neither. I am simply a man on a journey, carrying the burden not just of wood, but of the world's pain. Determination wells up within me, a fire igniting my spirit. I know what lies ahead, and though fear brushes against my heart, I push it aside. I am called to this moment, to embody love in the face of hatred, to demonstrate forgiveness in the midst of betrayal.

With each step, I lift my head a little higher. I am not alone; the presence of my Father surrounds me. I take a deep breath, feeling the strength of my mission, my heart beating with the rhythm of hope. I will carry this cross, not just for myself, but for every soul yearning for redemption.

The journey is long, and the road is steep, but I will not waver. I will embrace the path laid before me, for it is through this suffering that true love will shine. And as I continue to walk, I silently pray for those who watch, that they may one day understand the depth of this sacrifice.

The noise of the crowd swells around me, rising and falling like the tide. I hear shouts of "Crucify him!" mixed with the gasps of those who know me—who have witnessed the miracles, the compassion, and the love I have shared. Their voices weave through my thoughts, and I can't help but feel the weight of their expectations. I want to tell them that this isn't just about me; it's about all of us. It's about the love that binds us together, even when we stand divided.

As I stumble slightly under the cross's weight, I feel the rough wood pressing against my back, a constant reminder of my physical suffering. But in this moment, my mind drifts to the countless souls I've encountered. I think of the lepers I healed, the blind I gave sight to, and the outcasts I welcomed. Each face flashes before me like a precious memory—reminders of why I chose this path. I can almost hear their laughter, their cries of gratitude, their whispers of hope. I long to comfort the broken-hearted, to reach out to the lost and the weary. In my heart, I hold their pain alongside my own. I think of the woman caught in sin, the one who washed my feet with her tears; I remember the joy of restoring life to the dead, and the wonder in the eyes of those who believed. I wish I could tell them that my love will endure, even through this darkness.

With every step, I draw strength from the very act of walking this path. I am reminded that love is not just a feeling; it is an action, a choice made in the face of suffering. It is in the moments when it is hardest to love that true love reveals itself.

With every step, I feel an overwhelming wave of sorrow wash over me. I think of my disciples, the ones who followed me through storms and miracles, who sat with me at the Last Supper. I can feel their hearts breaking, each one grappling with the fear of losing me. My love for them runs deep, and I yearn to offer them reassurance, to tell them that they will find strength in the days to come.

My mind drifts to the teachings I've shared with them—lessons about love, sacrifice, and the call to serve. I recall the words I spoke about bearing one's own cross. In this moment, I realize that the very act of carrying this cross has become a powerful metaphor, not just for my own suffering, but for the burdens we all bear in life. Each of us carries our own weight, our own trials. I wish for them to understand that even in suffering, there is a path to redemption.

But even in this sorrow, there is a flicker of hope. I remember my promise to them: that I would not leave them alone, that I would send a comforter to guide them. I cling to this promise as I take each step, feeling the warmth of my Father's presence surrounding me.

As I approach the foot of the hill, I pause for a moment. The reality of what is about to happen weighs heavily in the air. I close my eyes, taking a deep breath, allowing the world around me to fade. I find solace in prayer, speaking quietly to my Father. "Let your will be done."

At that very moment, I inhale deeply, feeling the warmth of the sun on my face. I know what is to come—physical agony and emotional turmoil—but I also know that this sacrifice will lead to something greater. In this paradox, I find strength. My heart whispers a prayer, not just for myself, but for all those who will witness this moment. I pray that their hearts may open to love, that they may find understanding in this suffering.

In that very moment, I feel a profound sense of peace wash over me. This is my calling. This is my purpose. The pain I am about to endure will not be in vain. It will be a testament to love's power, a declaration that even in death, hope remains.

In that very moment, the reality of what lies ahead becomes clearer and nature seems to echo my reality. The wind rustles through the trees, carrying whispers of encouragement, while the sky above shifts, dark clouds gathering as if reflecting the weight of this moment. I sense the turbulence of the world, but I also feel the presence of hope breaking through, like sunlight piercing the gloom. In my heart, I cling to this vision—a world transformed by love, where forgiveness reigns, and every soul can find solace. As I look up at the sky, I feel the gentle touch of a breeze.

In that moment, I open my eyes, and I am ready. The road has been long, but each moment has led me here, and I will walk this final path with courage. For love will triumph over fear, and in my heart, I carry the promise of redemption for all.

The weight of the cross presses heavily on my shoulders as my thoughts drift to the prophecies that have long foretold this moment. I have spent my life walking in their shadows, guiding my disciples with the knowledge that my path was set by a greater plan, one that transcends time and understanding.

The words of Isaiah resonate deeply within me: "But he was pierced for our transgressions; he was crushed for our iniquities." I reflect on how these ancient words have woven through the fabric of my life. They speak of suffering and sacrifice, a promise that my pain will not be in vain. This is not just a personal journey; it is part of a divine narrative that reaches far beyond me.

I think of the countless times I've shared this message with my followers, how I've urged them to see beyond the immediate and embrace the deeper truths of love and redemption. Each miracle, every parable, every moment of compassion—these have all pointed toward the reality of this sacrifice. The punishment that brings peace is laid upon me, a weight I willingly bear.

As I struggle to walk, I can almost hear the whispers of the prophets who came before me, their voices echoing through time. They spoke of a suffering servant, one who would endure pain for the sake of others. In their words, I find both comfort and sorrow. I understand that this suffering is not just a mark of defeat; it is a pathway to healing—a chance for humanity to reconnect with the divine.

I feel the sharp edges of the wood digging into my flesh, a physical reminder of the torment that lies ahead. But I also feel an immense peace that washes over me. I am not alone in this. My Father walks beside me, and through this suffering, I can fulfill the promise of hope. The very act of my sacrifice will bridge the gap between the Creator and creation, allowing love to flow freely once more.

I think of those who have lost their way, who have been consumed by sin and despair. I bear their burdens now; I carry their grief and their longing for redemption. Each step I take is a step toward healing, not just for myself, but for all who have ever felt broken, lost, or abandoned.

The sun hangs low in the sky, casting a warm light that seems to pierce through the gloom of the day. I find solace in this light, a reminder of the hope that exists even in darkness. I remember the words of the psalmist: "Even though I walk through the darkest valley, I will fear no evil, for you are with me." This is my reality now; the darkness may surround me, but I know that I walk with the divine.

As I continue on this arduous journey, I reflect on how this suffering will bring about the very thing I have preached: love, reconciliation, and redemption. I think of the people I have encountered—each one a soul in need of grace. Their faces swirl in my mind, and I feel a deep sense of purpose rising within me. I am here for them, to demonstrate that even in the face of ultimate sacrifice, love remains steadfast and true.

I pause for a moment, looking out at the crowd gathered to witness this moment. I see the mixture of confusion, anger, and sorrow reflected back at me. I want to tell them that this is part of a greater story—a narrative of divine love woven into the fabric of existence. My heart aches for those who do not yet understand the significance of this moment. They see only a man being led to his death, but I see the fulfillment of hope—a new beginning for all.

The reality of Isaiah's prophecy settles in my heart. "By his wounds, we are healed." This isn't just a declaration of pain; it is a testament to the power of sacrifice. In this act of love, I will bear the sins of many, creating a path for them to return to the Father. It is a role I embrace fully, knowing that through this suffering, the world will come to know the depth of divine love.

As I take a deep breath, I am filled with a profound sense of peace. I know that my journey will lead to pain and separation, but I also trust in the promise of resurrection, the hope that will arise from the ashes of despair. This is the culmination of my mission, and I will face it with unwavering resolve. For in the end, love will triumph, and through my wounds, the world will be healed.

And so I press forward and the burden of the cross becomes almost a rhythmic pulse in my body, each step echoing the memories of a life lived in service and love. In these moments of pain, I find solace in recalling the faces of those I've encountered throughout my ministry—each one a testament to the purpose I have lived for.

I remember the day I walked through the village of Capernaum. The air was thick with anticipation, and the crowd surged toward me. A leper approached, his skin marred by the disease, a life cast aside by society. I can still feel the weight of his gaze, filled with desperation and hope. As I reached out to touch him, a hush fell over the crowd. "I am willing," I said, and in that moment, I witnessed the transformation—a healing that resonated not only in his body but in his very spirit. The joy that flooded his eyes is forever etched in my heart, a reminder of the power of compassion and the profound impact of simply being seen.

I think back to the Sermon on the Mount, where I spoke to the masses gathered on the hillside. I see their faces—some eager, some skeptical. I shared with them the Beatitudes, speaking of the blessedness of the poor in spirit, the mourners, and the meek. I remember the way their expressions shifted as my words took root in their hearts. "The Spirit of the Lord is on me," I had declared, feeling the weight of that truth. I sought to proclaim good news to the poor, to bring freedom to the prisoners, to offer recovery of sight to the blind. Each teaching was an invitation to a new way of seeing the world—a world transformed by love.

I recall the warmth of the fire as I shared meals with the outcasts and sinners—the ones society deemed unworthy. I remember Matthew, the tax collector, sitting at my table, his face initially etched with shame, but gradually softening as he realized he was accepted. The laughter that echoed around those tables was a melody of love, a testament to belonging. "It is not the healthy who need a doctor," I had said, "but the sick." In those moments, I felt the weight of my mission: to reach out to those who felt unloved, to show them that they were cherished in the eyes of God.

Each memory floods my mind like a vivid tapestry, woven together by the threads of joy, healing, and connection. I see the faces of the blind who regained their sight, the paralyzed who stood and walked, and the mourners who found hope in their grief. Each life touched, each heart opened, is a reflection of the divine love I sought to embody.

The impact of my ministry extends beyond these individual moments; it has sparked a movement of love and compassion that transcends boundaries. I think of the disciples who have followed me, who have taken my message into the world, spreading the seeds of hope I have planted. They carry my words and my spirit, and I find comfort in knowing that this journey will continue, even as I face the end of my earthly life.

I feel the warmth of the sun on my face, illuminating the path ahead, a reminder of the light I have tried to bring into the darkness. Even as I approach my crucifixion, I hold tightly to the belief that love cannot be extinguished. The legacy of my teachings will endure, igniting hearts and transforming lives long after I am gone.

As I stumble slightly, I catch a glimpse of a child watching from the sidelines, eyes wide with wonder. I see in him the hope of future generations, the potential for a world filled with love and understanding. I silently pray for him, that he may grow to embody the values I have shared—that he may continue to reach out to the marginalized, to speak truth to power, and to hold fast to the love that unites us all.

My memories of ministry are not merely reflections of the past; they are the foundation upon which my sacrifice stands. Each act of healing, each word of wisdom, each shared meal has built a bridge to this moment—a moment that will culminate in the greatest act of love. Though the road ahead is fraught with pain, I walk it knowing that every tear shed, every heart mended, and every life transformed will ripple through eternity.

In this moment of reflection, I realize that the purpose of my suffering is not an ending, but a continuation of the mission I began. This sacrifice will be the ultimate expression of love, an invitation for all to return to the embrace of the Father. And as I continue on this path, I carry with me the essence of my ministry—the profound belief that through love, we can heal, transform, and ultimately, find our way back home.

As I stumble onward, the weight of the cross presses harder against my shoulders, a relentless reminder of the sacrifice that lies ahead. With each labored step, I find myself lost in contemplation, reflecting on the profound significance of what it means to sacrifice for others.

Words echo in my mind: "Greater love has no one than this: to lay down one's life for one's friends." What does it truly mean to love in such a way? As I consider this, I realize that my entire ministry has been a preparation for this moment—a moment that embodies the ultimate act of love.

I think of the many who have crossed my path—the weary, the broken, the lost. Each person I encountered has added weight to my heart, a weight that now feels insurmountable. Each of them carries a piece of my heart, a connection forged in love and compassion.

To sacrifice oneself is to give up everything: comfort, security, and ultimately, life itself. I reflect on how love often demands such a price, how true love is not merely a sentiment but a call to action. It is a willingness to bear the burdens of others, to stand in the gap when they feel alone, and to offer oneself fully, even unto death.

In this moment, I understand that my sacrifice is not just for a select few; it is for all of humanity. I think of those who will come after me—the generations that will hear my teachings, who will seek solace in their suffering, and who will long for connection with the divine. I am laying down my life not only for my friends but for those who may not yet understand the depth of this love.

I feel a wave of sadness wash over me as I consider the pain that will ensue. The anguish of my disciples, the betrayal of Judas, the denial of Peter—all of it weighs heavily on my heart. Yet, I find a flicker of hope within that sorrow. In my act of selflessness, I will create a pathway for redemption, a bridge that will reconnect humanity with the heart of the Father.

I anticipate my final moments on the cross, how they will seem to the world. To many, I will appear as a failed Messiah, a man who came to save but ended up in defeat. But I know that this is not the end of the story. This sacrifice will echo through time, a powerful testament to the lengths I would go to demonstrate love.

I consider the phrase "lay down one's life." It is more than a physical death; it is a complete surrender to the will of God, an act of trust that transcends fear and doubt. It is an invitation for all to embrace vulnerability, to understand that love is often born out of pain and sacrifice.

As I walk, I envision the faces of those I love, those who will bear the weight of this loss. I hope they will remember my words, my teachings, and the love I have shared. I hope they will carry on the message of grace and forgiveness, that they will continue to reach out to those in need and create a community rooted in love.

The sun begins to set, casting a golden hue across the horizon. In this fading light, I feel a deep sense of peace settle over me. The journey I am on is fraught with suffering, yet I am not alone. I carry the hopes and dreams of humanity with me, and I know that this sacrifice will pave the way for a new beginning.

In the quiet of this moment, I offer a prayer of gratitude for the lives I have touched. Each person is a reflection of the love I have tried to embody, and I cherish the impact we have made together. My heart swells with a profound sense of purpose as I approach the culmination of my mission.

This weight of sacrifice is heavy, but it is also beautiful—a divine tapestry woven with threads of love, pain, and hope. And as I draw nearer to my destination, I know that I am ready to embrace this journey. I will lay down my life, not as an act of defeat, but as the ultimate expression of love, a love that will resonate through the ages, echoing in the hearts of all who seek the light.

With each difficult step the weight of the cross bears down on me like a storm cloud ready to break. With each agonizing step, my heart swells with a mixture of love and sorrow as I reflect on humanity—the beauty and the pain, the choices made and the paths taken.

I think of words I had spoke before, a lament for Jerusalem: "Jerusalem, Jerusalem, you who kill the prophets and stone those sent to you, how often I have longed to gather your children together, as a hen gathers her chicks under her wings, and you were not willing." This cry echoes in my soul, a reminder of the heartache that comes with rejection. I have poured myself into the lives of those I met, offering healing, hope, and the promise of love. Yet, so many have turned away, blind to the very essence of what I offer.

With every face I see in the crowd, I am reminded of the choices that define us. Some have chosen to follow, to embrace the light of my teachings, while others have chosen darkness, closing themselves off from the love that seeks to envelop them. It pains me to witness the division among my people—the ones who cling to the familiar, the ones who feel threatened by change. How often I have longed to gather them, to wrap them in the warmth of my love, to show them that there is always a way back to grace.

I reflect on the many moments shared with those who accepted my message. The joy in the eyes of the woman caught in adultery when I refused to condemn her, the gratitude of those who had been shunned by society—these memories fill my heart with warmth. Each act of compassion, every word of forgiveness, is a testament to the love that flows through me. Yet, for every soul I touched, there are countless others who remained distant, skeptical, unwilling to step into the embrace I offered.

I ponder the choices made by the leaders of my time, those who hold the power to influence and guide. Their rejection of my message, their fear of losing control, fills me with a profound sadness. They have sought to maintain the status quo, to protect their positions at the expense of the very people they are called to serve. It is a heart-wrenching irony that the very ones who should recognize the truth are often the first to turn away.

In this moment of reflection, I realize that love cannot be forced. It requires a willingness to open one's heart, to step beyond fear and doubt, and to embrace vulnerability. I have offered my life, my love, and my teachings as an invitation to a deeper relationship with the divine. Yet, ultimately, it is a choice that each person must make for themselves.

I look up to the sky, the fading light casting a soft glow over the city. The beauty of this moment reminds me of the divine potential within every individual. Each person is capable of great love, but they must choose to nurture that seed. I long to see them flourish, to witness them stepping into their true selves and embracing the connection that binds us all.

As I approach the hill of Golgotha, the final destination of this journey, I feel a swell of compassion for humanity. I know that my sacrifice will serve as both a beacon of hope and a mirror reflecting the choices they make. I will lay down my life so that they may understand the depth of love available to them—a love that forgives, a love that redeems, a love that ultimately triumphs over all.

I carry within me the collective heartbeat of humanity—the hopes, the fears, the struggles, and the triumphs. I know that even in the face of rejection, love will persist. It is a force that cannot be extinguished, a flame that burns brightly in the hearts of those willing to embrace it.

In these final moments, I hold tightly to the belief that my sacrifice will not be in vain. Though I may be met with disbelief and scorn, I trust that love will find a way to break through the barriers erected by fear and misunderstanding. I pray that my journey will awaken hearts and inspire a new way of living—one rooted in compassion, connection, and the profound truth that we are all children of the same Creator.

With each step, I move closer to the fulfillment of my mission. My love for humanity remains unwavering, a constant force that will guide me through the pain ahead. I will face this final act not with bitterness, but with the hope that one day, all will understand the depth of my commitment to them—a commitment that endures beyond death, lighting the way for all who seek to return home.

Suddenly, a wave of emotion crashes over me, a tumult of fear and determination intermingling as I steel myself for what is to come. The path has been fraught with trials and tribulations, and yet, in this moment, I feel an overwhelming sense of purpose enveloping me, guiding me toward the inevitable.

I pause for a moment, taking a deep breath to steady my heart. I recall the words I once spoke in the garden, a prayer that reverberates within me now: "Father, if you are willing, take this cup from me; yet not my will, but yours be done." The weight of those words resonates deeply as I confront the truth of my destiny. I feel the tension of my humanity, the desire to flee from pain and suffering, juxtaposed with the acceptance of the divine plan that unfolds before me.

In this inward dialogue, I surrender my will to the Father, trusting that there is a greater purpose at play. The anguish that courses through my veins is undeniable, yet I know that this journey is not just about me; it is about all

of humanity. Each moment of suffering I will endure serves a greater good, a chance for redemption, a path to salvation.
With each step toward the inevitable, I draw strength from the knowledge that I am not alone. The Father walks with me, His presence a comforting balm against the ache in my heart. I whisper a prayer of gratitude for the mission I have been given, for the love that has defined my life, and for the opportunity to fulfill the will of God.
In this moment of quiet resolve, I feel the weight of my purpose crystallizing. I am to be the bridge between heaven and earth, the embodiment of divine love made manifest in human form. I embrace this destiny, not as a burden, but as a gift—a chance to demonstrate the depths of love and the power of faith in the face of unimaginable suffering.
I close my eyes briefly, allowing the moment to envelop me. The sounds of the crowd fade into a distant murmur as I center my thoughts on the truth that will guide me through the pain: love is the answer. Love is the purpose. And love will always prevail.
As I stumble towards the hill of the hill of Golgotha, I hold onto the belief that this act of surrender will ripple through time, awakening hearts to the beauty of grace and the possibility of redemption. I am ready to embrace the path laid out before me, to fulfill the promise of hope that I have extended to all of humanity.
With a deep breath, I open my eyes and gaze upon the horizon, a sense of peace washing over me. I am walking into the unknown, but I do so with faith in God's plan and the unwavering knowledge that love, in all its forms, will carry me through.

Chapter 2: Foundations of Faith

As I stumble towards the hill of Golgotha, memories of my early life in Nazareth come flooding back, vivid and alive. The sights and sounds of that small, unassuming town are etched into my heart, each detail a thread in the tapestry of my existence.

Nazareth, nestled in the hills of Galilee, is a place where life unfolds in simple rhythms. The sun rises over the rugged terrain, casting warm golden light on the earthen homes scattered along the hillside. The air is filled with the scent of baked bread wafting from the ovens, mingling with the fragrant herbs that line the pathways. I can hear the laughter of children playing, the distant clanging of tools as fathers work in the fields, and the gentle murmur of mothers calling their little ones home.

Our family home is a modest structure, built of stone and clay, with a small courtyard where we gather for meals and share stories. The walls, though weathered, resonate with the laughter of my siblings and the gentle wisdom of my mother, Mary. I remember the way she would kneel beside me, teaching me the stories of our people—the tales of Abraham, Moses, and the prophets. Her voice, warm and nurturing, instilled in me a sense of belonging and purpose.

The market is a bustling hub of activity, filled with vibrant colors and the lively chatter of neighbors. I would often accompany my mother to barter for goods, her presence a soothing balm in the chaos. The vendors call out, their voices blending into a symphony of life. Fresh fruits and vegetables are laid out, their hues bright against the dusty stalls. I would gaze in wonder at the spices, their scents intoxicating, imagining the meals we would create together.

The synagogue stands at the heart of Nazareth, a place where my spirit felt both comfort and challenge. It is here that I first encountered the teachings of our faith, where I learned to read the scrolls and engage with the words of the prophets. I remember the hush that would fall over the congregation as the rabbi spoke, the reverence in the air palpable. Each lesson ignited a flame within me, stirring a hunger for understanding that would shape my journey. Every word of the rabbis resonated deeply, as they encapsulated the essence of my upbringing—a life steeped in love, faith, and community.

As I reflect on those early days, I am struck by the simplicity of life in Nazareth. There was beauty in the mundane, a sacredness in the routines of daily living. Family dinners filled with laughter, quiet moments of reflection by the evening fire, and the sense of belonging that enveloped me like a warm cloak—these are the memories that have shaped my understanding of love and compassion.

Yet, even in the midst of this idyllic existence, there were moments of awareness that hinted at a greater purpose. As I listened to the stories of our people, I began to recognize the weight of their struggles—the oppression under foreign rule, the longing for a promised deliverer, and the hope that flickered in the hearts of those who believed. It was a longing that resonated with my own spirit, stirring a sense of responsibility deep within me.

I remember the whispers of the townspeople as they spoke of the Messiah, a figure who would restore Israel and bring peace to our land. In those moments, a flicker of understanding ignited in my heart. Could it be that I was being called to something greater? A sense of destiny began to take root, though I was still a child, innocent and unassuming.

As I navigated my early years, I often found solace in the quiet of nature. The hills surrounding Nazareth were my refuge, a place where I could reflect on my thoughts and commune with the Creator. I would wander among the olive groves and listen to the rustling leaves, feeling a connection to something far beyond myself. In those moments, I sensed the presence of God, a gentle whisper guiding me toward my purpose.

In the simplicity of daily life, I began to understand the power of love and compassion. The acts of kindness I witnessed—neighbors helping one another, families caring for the sick, the sharing of food with those in need—were seeds planted in my heart. Each interaction reinforced the idea that love was not merely a word but a call to action, an invitation to serve and uplift those around me.

As I reminisce about my childhood in Nazareth, I am filled with gratitude for the foundation laid by my family and community. The values of love, faith, and service that were woven into the fabric of my upbringing would guide me as I ventured into the world, prepared to embrace the mission that awaited me.

In those early days, I learned that life is a tapestry of experiences, each thread contributing to a greater whole. The beauty of Nazareth—its sights, sounds, and the warmth of its people—has become a part of me, an indelible mark that will guide my steps as I fulfill the purpose for which I was born.

As I prepare to embrace my destiny, I carry with me the essence of those memories, a reminder of the love and compassion that define my mission. My journey is just beginning, but the lessons of my childhood will forever illuminate the path ahead.

The faces of my parents, Mary and Joseph, come vividly to mind. Their influence shaped me in profound ways, teaching me about love, faith, and the essence of family.

My mother, Mary, embodies nurturing in every sense. From the earliest days of my life, her warmth enveloped me like a soft blanket. I can still feel the gentle touch of her hands as she cradled me, singing lullabies that floated through the air like delicate whispers. Her faith was a beacon, illuminating the path of our family and infusing our home with a deep sense of purpose.

Mary taught me the importance of prayer, often leading our family in moments of gratitude and reflection. I remember her kneeling beside me, her voice steady and soothing, as she expressed our hopes and dreams to God. In those moments, I felt the sacredness of our bond, a connection that transcended the ordinary. Her wisdom shone brightly in the stories she shared, tales of our ancestors filled with lessons of courage, love, and resilience.

One of my favorite memories is of her gathering us around the evening fire, the flickering flames casting dancing shadows on the walls. She would recount stories of faith—how God guided our people through the wilderness, how He provided for them in times of need. Her eyes would sparkle with fervor as she spoke of the promise of a Messiah, planting seeds of hope and anticipation in my heart. I would listen, captivated, feeling the weight of those words as they settled into my soul.

In contrast, my father, Joseph, was a figure of steadfastness and strength. A humble carpenter, he embodied a work ethic that inspired me deeply. I watched him rise with the sun each day, his hands calloused yet gentle, shaping wood into forms that served our family and community. He taught me the value of diligence and integrity, instilling in me the belief that work is a sacred endeavor, a way to honor both family and God.

Joseph's love for Mary was evident in every interaction. He treated her with respect and tenderness, demonstrating what it means to be a partner in life. I learned from him that love is not just a feeling; it is an action, a commitment to support and uplift one another. His quiet strength provided a sense of security that allowed me to flourish in my own identity.

One vivid memory stands out: the day I saw him comforting Mary after a particularly difficult day. She had faced many years of ridicule from some in the town for the unusual nature of my birth as she bore the child in a manger; the child having been laid out in a trough that held hay for the farm animals. It was many years before I realized the child was me. Joseph, with his unwavering support, reassured her that their love was a divine gift. And in that moment, I witnessed the beauty of their partnership, a reflection of the love that God has for His people.

As I grew, I became increasingly aware of the unique role my parents played in my life. They were not just caregivers; they were mentors guiding me toward my purpose. I remember the quiet conversations we shared under the stars, where I would ask them about their hopes and dreams for me. Their responses were always filled with love and faith, encouraging me to embrace my destiny. He often recounted the time of my birth, emphasising that the angel of the Lord had commanded him to take Mary home as his wife and to have no union with her until she gave birth to me. This moment exemplifies the profound trust that my father placed in God's plan, demonstrating his commitment to both Mary and me.

My parents' unwavering faith became the cornerstone of my identity. They nurtured my spirit, encouraging me to seek a deeper understanding of God and my purpose. Together, they created a home filled with love, where faith flourished, and compassion was cultivated.

As I reflect on my upbringing, I see how vital their support was in nurturing my faith. In the fabric of our family life, I learned that love is the greatest teacher. It was through their examples that I began to grasp the importance of compassion and service to others, values that would guide me throughout my ministry.

In our quiet moments together, we would discuss the struggles of our people—the longing for liberation, and the search for hope. My parents instilled in me a sense of empathy, teaching me that our lives are interconnected and that we are called to serve one another. Their lessons became a lens through which I would later view the world, guiding my actions and decisions as I embarked on my mission.

In those formative years, I often found myself in prayer, seeking guidance and understanding. I remember the times I would sneak away to the olive groves, allowing the tranquility of nature to envelop me. It was there that I would reflect on my parents' teachings, seeking clarity on my purpose and the path that lay ahead.

Their love and faith formed the foundation upon which I would build my ministry. I am grateful for the sacrifices they made, for the lessons learned in the small moments of daily life. Their unwavering belief in me, in the divine purpose that surrounded us, ignited a flame within my heart—one that would carry me through trials and triumphs alike.

As I prepare to embrace my destiny, I carry with me the essence of their teachings—the importance of love, compassion, and unwavering faith. The lessons learned in the embrace of my family will forever guide me, serving as a compass as I step into the world, ready to fulfill the mission entrusted to me.

I falter beneath the burden, momentarily unsure. I hesitate, feeling the weight of my journey. In this stillness, I reflect.

In the heart of Nazareth, amidst the love of my parents, I found the roots of my identity. Their unwavering support and faith in God provided me with the strength to face the challenges ahead, reminding me that love is the greatest force of all, one that transcends time and space, uniting us in a divine tapestry of existence.

As I reminisce about my childhood in Nazareth, I remember moments that hinted at something greater, instances that made me feel different from my peers. In the simple joys of childhood—playing with friends, running through the fields, and laughing with my siblings—there was an undercurrent of awareness that set me apart. I often felt a pull toward deeper questions, an innate curiosity about the world and my place in it.

While other children were content to chase after games or listen to stories, I found myself drawn to quiet corners where I could ponder the mysteries of life. I would sit beneath the olive trees, feeling the warmth of the sun on my face, contemplating the stories my mother told me of our faith and the promises of God. In those moments of solitude, I sensed a profound connection to something beyond myself, a whisper that stirred my spirit.

One key experience stands out vividly, a moment that solidified my sense of purpose. It was the year I turned twelve, and my family made the pilgrimage to Jerusalem for the Passover festival. The city was alive with celebration, the air thick with the scent of incense and the sound of voices lifted in praise. I remember the excitement buzzing through me as we approached the temple, a place I had only heard about in stories.

Once in Jerusalem, the grandeur of the temple overwhelmed me. The towering stones, the intricate carvings, the throngs of worshippers—it was a sight that filled me with awe. I felt a magnetic pull toward the temple courts, where I could see scholars and teachers engaged in deep discussions about the Scriptures. My heart raced with an inexplicable yearning to be a part of that dialogue.

When my family prepared to leave after the festival, I stayed behind, drawn to the sacred space. My family thought I had travelled home alone, and for three days I immersed myself in conversations with the teachers, listening intently and asking questions that flowed from a place deep within me. The discussions were spirited, filled with wisdom that resonated in my soul. I remember feeling a sense of belonging there as if this was where I was meant to be.

It wasn't until my family finally returned to Jerusalem, frantically searching for me, that I understood the depth of their worry. When they found me in the temple, my mother's eyes were filled with relief and concern. "Son, why have you treated us like this?" she asked, her voice trembling. I looked into her eyes, sensing the weight of her love and anxiety. I responded simply, "Didn't you know I had to be in my Father's house?" In that moment, I realized the significance of what I had experienced. It was an awakening, a revelation of my divine purpose.

While my family saw me as their beloved son, I began to grasp that I was also part of a larger narrative—a mission that stretched far beyond the confines of our home in Nazareth. The teachers welcomed my questions, and as we exchanged ideas, I felt the words of the prophets come alive. I understood that I was not just a child; I was a vessel for God's message, a light meant to shine in a world yearning for hope.

This experience sparked a deep desire within me to explore my identity further. I began to reflect on the prophecies that foretold of a coming Messiah, and I sensed a stirring in my spirit, a connection to those ancient texts that transcended time. The stories of the past were not merely tales but promises waiting to be fulfilled.

In the following years, I often returned to those early reflections, grounding myself in the lessons of compassion, love, and the call to serve others. I realized that my journey would involve not only understanding my identity but also embracing the responsibility that came with it. As I grew, my interactions with others deepened my understanding of what it meant to love and serve—to heal the broken, to lift the weary, and to be a voice for the voiceless.

I learned that my awareness was not just about me; it was about the people around me. I would witness the struggles of my community—the poverty, the illness, the heartache—and I felt an urgency to act. I began to recognize that my purpose was intertwined with theirs; the call to love was a call to action.

With each passing day, I sought to embody the teachings I had absorbed from my parents and the wisdom of the Scriptures. I understood that my mission was not simply to fulfill prophecies but to demonstrate the love of God in tangible ways. The awareness of my divine purpose grew stronger, guiding my thoughts, actions, and prayers.

Now, as I prepare for what lies ahead, I carry with me the lessons learned from that pivotal trip to Jerusalem. My heart is filled with a sense of wonder and anticipation, knowing that I am on the cusp of a journey that will change not only my life but the lives of countless others. The awakening of my understanding of God's purpose for me is just the beginning, and I am ready to embrace the path laid out before me.

I stumble under the cross, pausing to catch my breath. In this fleeting moment, I reflect.

As I reflect on my childhood in Nazareth, I am reminded of the small acts of kindness that shaped my understanding of compassion and love. In the everyday moments spent with neighbors and the less fortunate, I found profound lessons that would later inform my teachings and mission.

Nazareth was a close-knit community, where everyone knew each other's names and stories. I recall many afternoons spent helping my neighbors with their daily tasks. Whether it was carrying heavy baskets of grain or tending to their gardens, these simple acts of service fostered a deep sense of connection within our community. I saw firsthand the joy that a helping hand could bring, and in those moments, I felt the essence of love—an unconditional willingness to support one another.

One particular memory stands out vividly. There was a widow in our neighborhood named Miriam, known for her kindness but burdened by the loss of her husband. Her home was modest, and often, I would see her struggling to make ends meet. One day, as I helped my mother prepare a meal, I felt a gentle tug at my heart. I urged my mother to make an extra portion and together we took it to Miriam's home.

When we arrived, I was met with a warmth that filled the small space. Miriam's eyes lit up as she welcomed us inside, and her gratitude poured forth like a gentle stream. "You have no idea how much this means to me," she said, her voice trembling with emotion. In that moment, I understood the impact of our actions—not just the meal, but the love behind it. It was in these experiences that I began to grasp the profound truth of words that often echoed in my mind: "Let the little children come to me, and do not hinder them, for the kingdom of God belongs to such as these.'"

Miriam's reaction reminded me of the sacredness of community and the importance of caring for one another. The love I felt in that moment ignited a fire within me—a desire to embody compassion and extend kindness to all. As I grew, I actively sought opportunities to serve those around me, whether it was helping a neighbor with their farm or comforting a friend in sorrow. Each act became a building block, shaping my understanding of love as a dynamic force that binds us together.

Another memorable encounter involved a group of children who often played near the well in our village. They were full of life and laughter, but I noticed that one child, a little girl named Sarah, often stood apart from the others. Her clothes were worn, and her face carried a hint of sadness. One day, I approached her, inviting her to join in our games. She hesitated at first, unsure of her place among us.

As we played, I took care to include her, offering her a share of the fun. Slowly, she began to smile, and the light in her eyes flickered back to life. That day, I learned that compassion often starts with inclusion, with recognizing those who feel left out. It was a simple gesture, yet it made a world of difference to

Sarah. Watching her joy filled my heart with a sense of fulfillment that went beyond mere happiness—it was a reflection of God's love in action.

In every encounter, I witnessed the power of kindness. I learned that love is not merely a feeling; it is a conscious choice to uplift others, to see the world through their eyes and offer a helping hand. Each experience became a lesson in empathy, teaching me that true compassion means acknowledging the struggles of others and responding with grace.

As I continued to observe the people of Nazareth, I became acutely aware of the challenges faced by many. I would see the elderly struggling to carry their burdens or the sick in need of care. I remember one evening when a storm swept through the village, damaging homes and leaving some families without shelter. My heart ached as I witnessed the devastation, and I knew I had to act.

The community came together, pooling resources and offering assistance to those in need. We worked side by side, repairing roofs and providing food. I took it upon myself to visit each family, ensuring they had what they needed. It was in these moments of collective love that I understood the essence of community—how our lives are woven together in a tapestry of shared experiences and mutual support.

Reflecting on these foundational experiences, I realize they deeply inform my later teachings on love and compassion. They became the lens through which I would view the world—a world in need of healing and understanding. As I prepare to embrace my purpose, I carry with me the lessons learned in the streets of Nazareth, where love was not just spoken but demonstrated in the simplest of actions.

In those early years, I felt a divine stirring within me, a recognition that my life was meant to be a reflection of God's love—a love that transcends barriers and embraces all. The stories of kindness and compassion I witnessed formed the bedrock of my understanding of what it means to serve others.

As I move forward on my journey, I am committed to embodying these principles, knowing that each act of love has the power to transform lives. My mission is clear: to extend the same compassion I received as a child, to reach out to the marginalized, the lost, and the broken, and to invite them into the embrace of divine love. The foundation laid in Nazareth will guide my footsteps as I strive to fulfill the purpose for which I was born.

I waver beneath the weight of my cross, taking a moment to steady my heart. In this stillness, I reflect.

As I stood on the threshold of adulthood, I found myself reflecting on the tapestry of experiences that had woven together to shape my identity. Each memory—each act of kindness, every lesson learned in the loving embrace of my family—had become a thread in the fabric of who I am. These early years in Nazareth were more than just a backdrop; they were the foundation upon which my mission is built.

Looking back, I see how each moment of compassion, each encounter with my neighbors, has deepened my understanding of love. The lessons imparted by my mother and father have resonated within me, guiding my thoughts and actions. Mary's nurturing spirit taught me the importance of empathy, while Joseph's steadfastness instilled in me a sense of responsibility and integrity. Together, they shaped my view of the world and the people within it.

I remember the joy in Miriam's eyes when I brought her food, and the way Sarah's laughter echoed through the air as she joined our games. These moments were not mere acts of charity; they were glimpses of the divine love that flows through all of creation. I began to recognize that each person carries a unique story, a journey filled with joys and sorrows, and it became my calling to honor those narratives.

As I contemplate my own journey, I feel a sense of urgency to share this message of belonging with others—to remind them that they, too, are beloved children of God. I understand that my identity is intricately linked to the experiences of my past. The kindness I have witnessed and the love I have shared would inform the way I engaged with the world. I was called to be a beacon of hope, to extend compassion to the marginalized, and to offer healing to the broken-hearted. My childhood experiences have equipped me with the tools necessary to fulfill this calling.

In these final moments of reflection, I realize that I was not merely stepping into adulthood; I was stepping into my purpose. The lessons of love, community, and service would guide my footsteps as I navigate the complexities of life. I was filled with a sense of anticipation, knowing that I am called to bring light to places shrouded in darkness.

My identity as a child of God is rooted in the love I have received and the love I am called to give. I see now that my mission is not simply about my own journey but about the collective journey of humanity. I am part of a larger story, one that transcends time and connects us all. The love that flows through me is not mine to keep; it is meant to be shared, multiplied, and woven into the lives of others.

The culmination of my childhood experiences has shaped my understanding of my mission. I am prepared to face the final challenge ahead, to embrace the suffering that comes with love, and to embody the message of hope that I carry. As I take these final steps into the future, I am filled with a deep sense of purpose—a purpose rooted in the very essence of who I am and who I am meant to be.

In these final moments of transition, I find peace in the knowledge that I am not alone. The love that has guided me thus far will continue to illuminate my path. My final journey is just the beginning; a mission that will blossom in the hearts of many.

Chapter 3: The Awakening of Purpose

I fumble. I rest. I reflect.

As I approach the banks of the River Jordan, the air is thick with anticipation. The landscape stretches before me, a tapestry of sun-drenched earth and vibrant greenery, the waters of the river glistening like jewels under the bright sun. The sound of rushing water mingles with the murmurs of the crowd gathered nearby—people drawn from all corners of Judea, their hearts stirred by the message of John the Baptist. I can feel their hopes, their struggles, and their yearning for redemption echoing in the air.

John stands in the water, a figure of wildness and purpose, his voice like thunder proclaiming a baptism of repentance. I observe the way he draws the people in, calling them to turn from their sins and prepare for the One who is to come. There is a raw authenticity in his message, a clarity that pierces through the noise of the world. Yet, as I watch, I am acutely aware of the weight of the moment before me.

Stepping into the cool water, I feel an overwhelming sense of humility wash over me. Here I am, the Son of Man, among the very people I have come to save, standing shoulder to shoulder with those who seek a new beginning. The water envelops my feet, sending ripples outward as I wade deeper, each step a symbol of my readiness to embrace this calling. It is more than a ritual; it is a profound act of submission, an acknowledgment of my mission to come.

As I kneel and allow myself to be immersed, the world around me fades. The water surrounds me, cradling me in its embrace. In that fleeting moment, I surrender myself fully—not just to the water, but to the purpose I have long felt stirring within me. I feel as if I am being washed clean, not of sins, but of any hesitations that may have lingered in my heart. Emerging from the depths, I take a breath, and with it comes a clarity I have not known before.

And then it happens. As I rise, shaking the water from my hair, the heavens above seem to part. A light, brighter than the sun, envelops me, and in that brilliance, I hear the unmistakable voice of my Father: "This is my Son, whom I love; with him, I am well pleased." The words resonate deep within my soul, igniting a fire of purpose that courses through my veins.

In that moment, I am filled with an overwhelming sense of affirmation. This is not just a moment of personal significance; it is a divine confirmation of my mission on earth. My heart swells with love, knowing that my Father sees me, knows me, and supports me in this journey ahead. The joy of that declaration mingles with the weight of responsibility that comes with it. I am being called to lead, to teach, and to heal—a charge that is both exhilarating and daunting.

Reflecting on the significance of this moment, I recognize that it marks the beginning of my ministry. The path ahead is fraught with challenges, but I am reminded that I do not walk it alone. The support of my Father will be my guiding light, illuminating even the darkest corners I may encounter. With this affirmation, I feel empowered to face the trials that lie ahead.

Yet, even amid this profound moment, I also sense the doubts that accompany such a calling. Am I truly ready for what lies ahead? Can I fulfill the expectations that will surely be placed upon me? The voices of those who doubt, the criticisms that will come, already begin to echo in my mind. But in the stillness of that moment, I realize that my Father's love is greater than any fear I may hold. I am reminded that it is not my own strength that will carry me, but His love and guidance.

As I step back onto the shore, I am met with the eager faces of the crowd, some still gazing at me with wide eyes, while others return to their conversations. The moment of my baptism will ripple through their lives in ways I cannot yet understand. I look into their eyes, sensing the hunger for truth and connection. I am reminded that my ministry is not just about me; it is about them—the broken, the lost, and the seeking.

This transformative moment at the River Jordan is more than a personal milestone; it is a clarion call to embrace the journey ahead. With each step I take from this place, I carry the weight of my Father's words with me, a reminder that I am called to love and to serve, to heal and to guide. The path of ministry is unfolding before me, and with it, the realization that every act of love, every teaching, and every moment of connection will be an extension of this divine affirmation.

As I continue my journey, I hold tight to this moment—the water, the light, and the voice that proclaimed my identity. It will serve as a beacon in times of uncertainty, reminding me of the purpose that has been bestowed upon me. With a heart full of hope and determination, I embrace the mission that awaits, ready to step into the lives of those I am called to touch. The adventure of ministry has begun, and I am poised to follow the path laid out before me, guided by the love and affirmation of my Father.

As I reflect further on that transformative moment at the River Jordan, I find my thoughts drifting back to the faces of those who gathered there. Each person was a tapestry of stories, hopes, and struggles, and I wonder how my journey will intersect with theirs. The anticipation in their eyes speaks of a longing for something greater—perhaps they too seek healing, redemption, or simply a glimpse of the divine in their everyday lives.

The voices of the crowd fade into the background as I contemplate the magnitude of the calling I have just accepted. It is one thing to feel the stirring of a mission within me, but quite another to recognize the responsibility that comes with it. The words of my Father still echo in my mind, a reminder that I am not just a messenger but His Son, imbued with purpose. What does that mean for me as I step into this role? How can I best embody the love and grace He has shown me?

As I walk away from the riverbank, I carry the warmth of the sun on my skin, a symbol of the light I hope to bring into the world. The path ahead is uncertain, filled with twists and turns that I cannot yet see. Yet, I know that every step I take will be guided by the affirmation I have received. I resolve to be present with those I encounter, to listen deeply, and to love fiercely, reflecting the essence of my Father's heart.

In the days that follow, I feel a magnetic pull toward those who are suffering, the outcasts and the marginalized. I remember the faces of the sick, the poor, and the broken-hearted. Each encounter reminds me of the lessons I learned during my childhood in Nazareth—lessons about compassion, kindness, and the beauty of community. These teachings form the foundation of my ministry, shaping my understanding of what it means to truly love others.

I recall the moments spent with Mary and Joseph, my earthly parents, who instilled in me the values of humility and service. Their unwavering faith in God's plan for our family serves as a model for my own journey. I realize that my ministry will not just be about grand gestures or miracles; it will also be about the everyday acts of love that often go unnoticed. The small moments of connection—sharing a meal with a hungry child, comforting a grieving widow, or simply offering a listening ear—are where the true power of love manifests.

As I begin to share my message, I find myself drawn to the teachings that resonate deeply within me and focus my life on very specific blessings: the Beatitudes. The Beatitudes become a guiding framework for my ministry, articulating the heart of my message: blessed are the poor in spirit, those who mourn, the meek, and the merciful. I realize that these teachings offer hope to the downtrodden and remind them of their inherent worth in the eyes of God. My mission is to elevate the voices of those who have been silenced, to bring light to their struggles, and to help them see the beauty within themselves.

Each encounter I have with my followers deepens my understanding of the transformative power of love. I see how the simplest acts—a touch, a kind word, a shared moment of vulnerability—can heal wounds that run deep. It becomes clear to me that my role is not to impose my will but to invite others into a relationship with the divine, to guide them toward the love that is available to all.

Yet, amid the excitement of this new beginning, I am also acutely aware of the challenges that lie ahead. I know that my message will not always be received with open arms. There will be those who challenge my authority, who misunderstand my intentions, and who cling to the very systems I aim to transform. The path of ministry will demand resilience and courage, a willingness to face rejection and criticism.

In these moments of doubt, I return to the river, to the voice that affirmed my identity. I remember that I am not alone in this journey; the love of my Father is my anchor. With each encounter, I am reminded of the importance of faith—not just in God but also in the goodness of humanity. I believe that love has the power to break down barriers and that, through my ministry, I can help others see the divine light within themselves.

As I prepare for the ministry ahead, I find solace in prayer, seeking guidance and strength. I reflect on the many moments that have led me to this point and the people I have met along the way. I am filled with gratitude for the opportunity to serve, to share the good news of love and redemption, and to walk alongside those who seek hope in their lives.

With each passing day, I feel more grounded in my purpose. The call to ministry is not merely a title; it is an invitation to embody the very love that created the universe. It is a chance to be a vessel for healing, to inspire change, and to foster a sense of community that transcends boundaries.

As I continue to walk this path, I hold tightly to the affirmation I received at my baptism. It is a reminder that my identity is rooted in love, and that the journey ahead, while daunting, is also filled with the promise of transformation. I step forward, ready to embrace the mission that awaits, knowing that the heart of my ministry will always be love—love for my Father, love for myself, and love for all those I encounter along the way.

As I step into the world of ministry, the excitement and trepidation mingle within me, fueling my every step. The moment I emerged from the waters of the Jordan, I knew that my journey would not be traveled alone. I was called not just to share a message, but to cultivate a community—a family of followers who would walk with me, learn from me, and, in turn, teach others about the love that God has for all.

It begins on the shores of the Sea of Galilee, where the sun casts a warm glow over the waters, and fishermen toil tirelessly in their boats. It is here that I first encounter Peter and Andrew, brothers who have dedicated their lives to the sea. Their hands are rough from labor, their faces weathered, yet their spirits are vibrant and hopeful. As they haul in their nets, I approach them, sensing a divine connection that transcends the ordinary.

"Come, follow me," I invite, my voice calm yet resolute. "I will send you out to fish for people."

The simplicity of my words hangs in the air, and for a moment, there is silence. Andrew glances at Peter, his eyes wide with wonder. I can see the flicker of doubt in their expressions—what would it mean to leave everything behind? Yet, in that moment, they also sense something greater at play, a calling that resonates deep within their souls.

Without hesitation, they drop their nets and follow me, their faces lit with a mix of astonishment and exhilaration. It is a pivotal moment—not just for them, but for me as well. I am reminded of the significance of community, of how the bonds we form can propel us toward our shared purpose. Peter and Andrew will become my first disciples, and together we will create a tapestry of faith woven from our diverse experiences and backgrounds.

Soon after, I encounter James and John, the sons of Zebedee, mending their nets by the shore. They are strong and spirited, with a fire in their hearts that matches the intensity of their labor. When I call to them, they respond with an eagerness that warms my heart. The moment is electric, filled with potential and promise. They, too, leave their father behind and join our growing band of followers.

Each of these encounters reinforces the importance of connection and community in my ministry. I recognize that building relationships is not merely about numbers; it is about forming a family united in our quest for love and understanding. These men, with their strengths and weaknesses, will become my companions in this journey, each one bringing unique gifts that will enrich our mission.

As we walk together, I take time to share the teachings that will define our collective path. I speak of love—love for God, love for one another, and love for our neighbors. I emphasize the significance of compassion, urging my followers to see the divine spark in every person they encounter. Together, we explore the idea that true greatness lies not in power or status, but in humility and service.

"Whoever wants to be my disciple must deny themselves and take up their cross daily and follow me," I remind them, drawing upon the truth that discipleship requires sacrifice. The path we tread will not always be easy, but I assure them that it is paved with purpose. Each teaching I share becomes a stepping stone toward a deeper understanding of our shared mission.

One day, as we sit in a circle under the shade of a tree, I invite the disciples to share their thoughts and feelings. I want to foster an environment where openness flourishes, where questions can be asked without fear of judgment. It is in these moments of vulnerability that our bonds deepen, allowing us to explore our collective faith in a safe space.

"Why do you choose to follow me?" I ask, looking each of them in the eye. Their answers vary—some speak of the hope I bring, while others share their desire for change in their lives. Each response adds to the fabric of our community, weaving a narrative of shared dreams and aspirations.

As I witness their growing camaraderie, I reflect on the beauty of this journey we are embarking on together. Each disciple is a unique thread in this tapestry, their lives intertwined with mine, and together we will weave a story of faith that will echo through generations.

In the days that follow, we travel from village to village, sharing our message of love and compassion with anyone willing to listen. I teach them about the Kingdom of God, a realm where the last shall be first, and the meek shall inherit the earth. These teachings resonate deeply with the people we encounter, and I watch as the seeds of faith take root in their hearts.

With each passing moment, I see the transformative power of connection. We gather the outcasts, the marginalized, and the forgotten. As we share meals with them, heal their wounds, and offer words of encouragement, I am reminded of the essence of my mission. It is not enough to preach from a distance; I must engage, connect, and embody the love I speak of.

In those early days, I also experience the challenges of building a community. There are moments of tension and disagreement among my disciples. As they learn and grow, they bring their differing perspectives and personalities to the table. I welcome these moments, knowing that they are essential for our growth. Each conflict is an opportunity for deeper understanding, a chance to practice forgiveness and grace.

Through it all, I remain committed to fostering a sense of belonging among us. I teach them about the importance of empathy, urging them to see the world through the eyes of others. It is in this shared journey of faith that we begin to realize the profound truth: we are not just followers of a teacher; we are co-creators of a community rooted in love.

As we share these early teachings, I can sense the excitement building within my disciples. They begin to understand the weight of the mission we share, and their hearts swell with anticipation for what is to come. Together, we are not just a collection of individuals; we are a family bound by a common purpose.

And so, as we move forward, I hold tight to the lessons learned in those early encounters. The significance of community will be a guiding principle throughout our journey. It is within this bond that we find strength, resilience, and an unwavering commitment to our shared mission of love.

I know that the road ahead will be filled with both triumph and tribulation. But in these early days, surrounded by my first disciples, I feel a profound sense of hope and gratitude. Each moment spent together is a reminder of the power of connection, the beauty of love, and the transformative potential of community. As we journey further, the early encounters with my followers shape not only their understanding of my mission but also mine. The landscape around us becomes a backdrop for profound teachings, moments of connection, and the cultivation of faith.

In the weeks that follow, our group expands as we draw more people into our fold. Each encounter brings new personalities, stories, and struggles, enriching our collective experience. We meet individuals from diverse backgrounds—fishermen, farmers, tax collectors, and even those deemed unclean by society. This diversity is a reflection of the Kingdom I speak of, a place where all are welcome, and love knows no boundaries.

One day, while walking along the shore, I come across Matthew, a tax collector. His presence stirs a mix of emotions within the people around me. He is a man of wealth but also one of disdain among his peers. As I approach him, I feel the weight of judgment hanging in the air, but I am unyielding. "Follow me," I say, my voice steady and inviting.

The shock in the eyes of my disciples is palpable. How can I call this man, a symbol of betrayal, into our circle? Yet, I know that grace is often found where it is least expected. Matthew hesitates for a moment, torn between his old life and the new path I offer. But ultimately, he rises, leaving behind his post and joining our ranks.

With Matthew's addition, our community grows richer in its complexity. I take time to engage with each of my followers individually, learning their stories and understanding their hearts. In these moments, I see the struggles they face—the burdens they carry, the hopes they cherish. I emphasize the importance of love and acceptance, encouraging them to see beyond labels and societal norms.

As we gather for meals, I share parables that resonate deeply with my followers. One evening, seated under the stars, I recount the story of the Good Samaritan. I watch as their faces light up with understanding. "Who is my neighbor?" I ask, echoing the question that sparked this teaching. The answer unfolds before us as we discuss our responsibilities to one another, the call to love that transcends cultural and societal divides.

It becomes clear that my message is taking root. The teachings of love, compassion, and acceptance resonate with my followers, and I see their hearts begin to open. They start to embody the very principles I preach, reaching out to the marginalized in their own communities, offering assistance and companionship.

As our ministry flourishes, I also encounter moments of doubt—both within myself and among my disciples. The weight of my calling often feels immense, and I find myself wrestling with questions about my mission and the path ahead. My disciples, too, sometimes struggle with uncertainty. They look to me for guidance, seeking reassurance in moments of vulnerability.

During one such moment, I gather them together, sensing their apprehension. "It's normal to feel doubt," I tell them. "Even in moments of uncertainty, we must hold fast to our purpose. Love is our anchor, and together we can weather any storm."

I encourage them to share their fears, creating an atmosphere of trust where honesty can flourish. In these discussions, I emphasize that our journey is not one of perfection but of growth. Each stumble and misstep is an opportunity to learn and deepen our faith.

In the quiet moments, I reflect on the weight of the mission ahead. I remember the voice of affirmation from my baptism, echoing in my mind: "This is my Son, whom I love; with him, I am well pleased." It serves as a reminder of the divine support I carry with me, even in the face of challenges. I am not alone in this journey; my followers stand beside me, united in our quest to spread love and compassion.

As we prepare for the next phase of our ministry, I recognize that each encounter has molded us into a community defined by purpose. The excitement among my followers is palpable, and I feel a renewed sense of energy coursing through our group. We are not merely a collection of individuals; we are a movement, a family bound by a shared mission to embody the love of God.

Together, we venture forth to heal the sick, embrace the outcasts, and share the message of hope. Each miracle we perform, each lesson we teach, brings us closer to understanding the true nature of the Kingdom we seek to build.

In the coming days, we will face challenges, opposition, and moments of doubt. But I know that the bonds we've formed will be our strength. The love we share will guide us through the darkest valleys, and together, we will continue to spread the light of compassion and grace.

As I look around at my disciples, their faces filled with hope and determination, I am filled with gratitude. This journey is not just mine; it belongs to all of us. Together, we will weave a narrative of love that will echo throughout history, transforming hearts and lives along the way.

And so, as we prepare to step into the world, I carry with me the lessons learned from these early encounters. The foundation of our community is built on love, compassion, and the unwavering belief that together, we can make a difference. With each step we take, I am reminded that we are not just sharing a message; we are living it. The call to ministry is a call to action, a call to embody the love of God in every interaction, and I am ready to embrace the journey ahead, hand in hand with my beloved disciples.

Pain. I lose my footing. I breathe deeply. I reflect.

I recall stepping into the days of my ministry, a complex tapestry of emotions unfolds within me. There are moments of soaring excitement, tempered by deep currents of doubt. Each morning, as I rise to greet the sun, I feel a mixture of anticipation and apprehension. This path is both exhilarating and daunting, a journey that promises to challenge my spirit and test my resolve.

The early encounters with my followers have ignited a fire within me. Each face I see reflects a yearning for connection, for understanding, for healing. The joy of sharing my message fills my heart; I long to bring hope to those in despair, to illuminate the darkness that often shrouds their lives. Yet, as the days progress, I find myself grappling with the weight of expectation.

What if I fail? What if the words I share do not resonate, or worse, if they lead people astray? The responsibilities weigh heavily on my shoulders. I think of the voices of the prophets who came before me, the burdens they bore, and the price they paid. Their stories echo in my mind, reminding me that the path of truth is rarely easy.

As I walk through the bustling streets of Galilee, I observe the world around me—the farmers tending to their fields, the children laughing in the dust, the elderly sharing stories under the shade of trees. Each moment is a reminder of the beauty of life, yet also of the suffering that permeates it. I am moved by the plight of those who struggle, and it stirs something deep within me, a longing to reach out and touch their lives.

In quiet moments, I retreat to the hills, seeking solace in the embrace of nature. The expansive sky above me feels like a canvas, and I often lift my gaze, searching for guidance. "Father," I whisper, "grant me clarity in the midst of uncertainty." The wind rustles through the leaves, a gentle reminder that I am not alone. These moments of prayer ground me, anchoring my spirit in the face of doubt.

It is during one such moment that I encounter a profound realization: doubt does not diminish my faith; rather, it can coexist with it. My uncertainty becomes a catalyst for deeper understanding. As I wrestle with my fears, I find my faith growing stronger, more resilient. I recall the voice from the heavens at my baptism, affirming my identity and purpose. That divine declaration is a light that guides me through the shadows of uncertainty.

With each encounter I have with my followers, I am reminded of the excitement that accompanies new beginnings. I see their eager faces, filled with hope and a thirst for truth. When I speak, I feel their energy flowing back to me, igniting my spirit. The thrill of sharing my message, of connecting with those who seek something greater than themselves, electrifies the air.

There are times when I share stories—parables that encapsulate the essence of love, compassion, and the radical nature of the Kingdom. As I weave these tales, I see the glimmer of understanding in their eyes. The excitement of these moments is palpable; together, we create a sacred space where hope flourishes and hearts open. I realize that my mission is not just to teach but to cultivate a community where love can thrive.

Yet, even amidst the joy of new connections, doubts whisper in my ear. What if I mislead them? What if my message is misunderstood? In the stillness of night, I lay awake, the weight of these thoughts pressing down on me. I recall the words of the prophets, their own struggles with doubt and fear, and I find solace in their experiences. They, too, faced the unknown, yet remained faithful to their calling.

It is in these moments of vulnerability that I am met with encouragement from my followers. They share their own struggles, their own fears, and in doing so, we create a bond forged in honesty. I encourage them to voice their doubts, to share their questions, for it is in dialogue that we grow. Together, we navigate the complexities of faith, and I realize that our shared journey brings us closer to understanding the divine.

In our gatherings, we celebrate small victories—acts of kindness, moments of healing, shared laughter. Each triumph becomes a testament to our collective faith. I witness the transformation in my followers as they embrace the teachings of love and compassion. The growth fills me with hope, reinforcing the belief that together, we can make a difference in the world.

As the days turn into weeks, I embrace the duality of my journey—the excitement of new beginnings intertwined with the reality of doubt. I recognize that both elements are essential to my growth. The exhilaration propels me forward, while the uncertainties keep me grounded, reminding me to seek guidance and remain humble.

One evening, gathered around a fire with my disciples, I share my heart. "Doubt is not the enemy; it is a part of our journey. In our struggles, we find strength, and in our questions, we discover truth." I see their faces illuminated by the flickering flames, and I know that my words resonate. We are not just a group of followers; we are a family bound by faith and love.

With each passing day, I embrace my calling with renewed vigor. I am more than a teacher; I am a guide, a friend, and a beacon of hope for those who seek it. The excitement of sharing my message fuels my spirit, while the reality of doubt reminds me to lean into faith. Together, we will navigate the unknown, embracing the journey with open hearts and unwavering courage.

As we prepare to face the challenges that lie ahead, I am filled with a profound sense of purpose. The path may be fraught with uncertainty, but I know that love will light our way. Each step we take, each soul we touch, is a testament to the transformative power of faith.

And so, as we venture forth into the world, I carry with me the lessons learned in this season of my ministry—the beauty of connection, the strength found in vulnerability, and the unwavering belief that together, we can create a tapestry of love that reflects the heart of God.

I am so tired. The splinters from the cross piece my skin. I hesitate. I gather my thoughts.

As I embark on this journey of ministry, I find myself reflecting deeply on the core messages that will shape not only my teachings but also the very fabric of my relationships with those who seek to follow me. The essence of my mission is woven from love, forgiveness, and humility, and I am filled with a sense of urgency to share these truths with the world.

At the heart of my message lies love—a love that transcends boundaries and expectations. It is not merely an emotion but a call to action, a way of being that invites others to experience the divine in their lives. I recall the Beatitudes, those beautiful pronouncements that express the heart of the Kingdom: "Blessed are the poor in spirit, for theirs is the kingdom of heaven" Each line encapsulates the values of the Kingdom, where the marginalized are honored, and the meek are elevated.

As I speak these words, I see the faces of those who gather around me. Many are weary from the burdens of life, their spirits heavy with sorrow and regret. I want them to know that in their vulnerability, they are not forgotten. My heart aches for the broken, and I share these teachings not as a set of rules but as an invitation to embrace a new way of living. The poor in spirit, the mourners, the meek—they all have a place in this divine narrative.

Forgiveness is another pillar of my message. In a world rife with conflict and division, the ability to forgive is revolutionary. I want to teach my followers that forgiveness is not a sign of weakness but a profound strength. It is the pathway to healing, both for the one who forgives and the one who is forgiven. "For if you forgive other people when they sin against you, your heavenly Father will also forgive you" In sharing this message, I am challenging them to embrace vulnerability and to see forgiveness as a transformative act.

Humility, too, is crucial. In a society that often values power and status, I seek to flip that narrative on its head. True greatness comes not from position but from service. "Whoever wants to become great among you must be your servant" I reflect on the profound implications of this teaching, recognizing that it requires a complete reorientation of how we understand worth and dignity.

In many ways, my approach to spirituality is revolutionary. I find myself contrasting the rigid structures of religious norms with a more personal relationship with God. The law has its place, but it should never overshadow the spirit of love and grace. I see the faces of the Pharisees, those who cling tightly to tradition, often missing the heart of the message. They emphasize adherence to the law, but I want my followers to understand that God desires mercy, not sacrifice.

In my teachings, I emphasize that spirituality is not confined to rituals or religious observances; it is an intimate relationship with the divine. "I am the way and the truth and the life" is more than a statement; it is an invitation to know God personally. I long for my followers to experience this relationship as one that is alive, vibrant, and transformative.

My methods for teaching reflect this emphasis on personal connection. I often use parables—simple stories that convey deep truths. They are accessible to all, inviting listeners to engage their hearts and minds. Through these stories, I hope to illuminate the complexities of faith and the nature of God's love. Each parable serves as a mirror, reflecting the hearts of those who listen and encouraging them to see themselves within the narrative.

In my interactions, I strive for authenticity. I engage in direct conversations, meeting individuals where they are. Whether it is a woman at the well or a tax collector perched in a tree, I want them to know that their stories matter. I listen, I ask questions, and I create a space for genuine dialogue. In doing so, I cultivate an environment where vulnerability is welcomed, and transformation is possible.

Prayer and contemplation are central to my own journey as well. In quiet moments, I retreat to the mountains or the gardens to connect with God. It is there that I find clarity and strength. The practice of prayer grounds me, reminding me of the purpose behind my mission. I want my followers to know that prayer is not merely a ritual but a conversation with the Creator. It is in those still moments that I receive the wisdom and guidance needed to lead.

I envision prayer as a lifeline, connecting us to the divine and to one another. In my teachings, I will emphasize its importance, encouraging others to cultivate a rich prayer life. I want them to see prayer as an opportunity for intimacy with God, a chance to lay bare their hopes, fears, and dreams. It is in these moments of communion that our spirits are renewed, and our paths clarified.

As I continue to define these key teachings, I feel a deep sense of responsibility to embody them. My life must reflect the love, forgiveness, and humility that I advocate. I understand that my actions will speak louder than my words, and I am determined to walk the path I invite others to follow.

In this unfolding journey, I recognize that the essence of my ministry is not only in what I teach but in how I live. I am called to be a vessel of love, a beacon of hope, and a catalyst for change. The teachings I share will take root in the hearts of my followers, and together, we will embark on a journey that transcends the ordinary and touches the divine.

With each lesson learned and each connection forged, I am reminded that this ministry is not solely about me; it is about us—this beautiful tapestry of souls coming together to experience the fullness of life in God. I embrace the call to guide, to inspire, and to love fiercely, knowing that our shared journey has the power to transform the world.

I hesitate, the air thick with sorrow, and I breathe deeply, grounding myself. In this precious pause, I reflect on the love I've given, the lessons learned, and the journey ahead.

As I reflect on the journey that has brought me to this moment, a deep sense of purpose washes over me. Each experience—my baptism, the encounters with my early followers, and the teachings I've begun to share—has woven together to solidify my identity as the Messiah. It is as if each thread of my life has been pulled taut, revealing a divine design that is both beautiful and daunting.

The affirmation I received at the River Jordan echoes in my heart: "This is my Son, whom I love; with him, I am well pleased" Those words are more than mere echoes; they are a clarion call to embrace the mission set before me. In these early days of my ministry, I feel the weight of expectation, not just from the people but from the divine. I am reminded that I am here not just to perform miracles or teach profound truths, but to embody the very love and grace of God.

In the quiet moments of reflection, I can see how my encounters with my first disciples have shaped me. Their eager faces and heartfelt questions inspire me. They remind me that my teachings must resonate deeply with their lives. This sense of community is vital; it is a foundation upon which we will build a movement rooted in love, compassion, and understanding. I envision a fellowship that embraces all—those who are broken, marginalized, and lost. I want to create a space where they can encounter the divine in ways that transform their lives.

The teachings that are beginning to take shape within me are revolutionary. I envision a world where love transcends law, where forgiveness dismantles barriers, and where humility redefines greatness. These teachings are not merely theoretical; they are deeply personal. They resonate with my own struggles and triumphs, my own experiences of joy and pain. As I share them, I feel a deep connection to those who are listening, a sense that we are embarking on this journey together.

Looking ahead, I feel a mixture of anticipation and trepidation. The road before me is fraught with challenges, yet it is also illuminated with the promise of joy and transformation. I know that the path will not be easy. There will be moments of doubt, resistance, and even rejection. But in my heart, I carry the assurance of my purpose—a purpose that is greater than myself.

The thought of confronting the authorities, challenging societal norms, and revealing the heart of God to those who have lost their way both excites and terrifies me. I am aware that my message will not always be welcomed; it may provoke anger and fear. But I am compelled by a greater love that propels me forward. The urgency of my mission fills me with resolve. I will speak truth to power, and I will stand with the oppressed.

As I prepare for the journey ahead, I seek solace in prayer. I return to the quiet places where I can lay bare my fears and hopes before God. In those sacred moments, I am reminded of the importance of grounding myself in the divine. It is through prayer that I find strength and clarity, that I am renewed and reoriented. I pray not only for myself but for those who will walk alongside me. I pray for my disciples, that their hearts may be open to the truths we will uncover together.

I also feel a sense of gratitude for the experiences that have shaped me thus far. My childhood in Nazareth, the love of my family, and the lessons learned from the people I have encountered have all played a crucial role in my formation. Each moment has prepared me for this calling, and I recognize the divine hand at work in my life.

As I look to the future, I envision a tapestry of stories yet to be written—a narrative filled with healings, teachings, and encounters that will change lives. I see the faces of those who will be transformed by the message of love and grace. I anticipate the joy of sharing meals with those on the margins, the laughter of children as they gather around me, and the profound moments of connection that will bridge the gaps of separation.

In the depths of my heart, I hold a profound hope: that the message I carry will not only resonate in the hearts of my followers but will ripple out into the world, igniting a movement of love that transcends time and space. This is not merely a personal journey; it is a collective awakening to the divine presence that permeates all of creation.

With this understanding, I stand ready to embrace the unfolding of my mission. I am prepared to walk the path of the Messiah, to embody the love of God in every word spoken and every action taken. As I move forward, I carry with me the conviction that I am not alone. The divine purpose that has been laid upon my heart is a guiding light, illuminating the way through the challenges that lie ahead.

The emergence of the Messiah is not merely a title; it is a call to action, a commitment to love fiercely and unconditionally. I am here to reveal the heart of God, to offer hope to the hopeless, and to invite all into a relationship that transforms lives. I am ready to step into the fullness of my identity, knowing that I am a vessel for the divine love that seeks to flow into the world.

As I prepare to embark on this journey, I take a deep breath, feeling the weight of the cross ahead. But I am buoyed by the love that surrounds me, and I am eager to share this love with all who will listen. The journey of ministry has just begun, and with it, the unfolding of a new chapter in the story of humanity—a story that will echo through the ages.

Nausea swells within me, pain courses through my body, making each breath a struggle. Yet, amid this torment, I find space to reflect on love, sacrifice, and the purpose of my suffering.

As I pause to reflect on all that has transpired, the weight of my mission settles deeply within me. This journey is not merely a personal endeavor; it is a shared path woven together with the faith of those who walk alongside me. In this moment, I recognize the profound importance of faith, community, and love as the foundational elements that will guide us through the challenges ahead.

Faith is the light that illuminates the darkest corners of our hearts. It is the assurance that we are never alone, even when the road seems daunting. I feel the presence of the divine, a constant reminder that my steps are guided by a higher purpose. In the quiet whispers of my soul, I hear the echoes of encouragement, urging me to trust in the plan that has been set before me. This faith is not blind; it is born from the experiences I have gathered and the affirmations I have received.

Community, too, is a vital thread in this tapestry. The disciples who have chosen to follow me bring their own stories, struggles, and dreams. Each one contributes a unique perspective that enriches our shared experience. Together, we will create a fellowship rooted in love and acceptance, a sanctuary for those who feel lost or marginalized. It is within this community that we will find strength and resilience, supporting one another as we navigate the complexities of life and faith.

Love is the essence that binds us all. It is the driving force behind every teaching I share, every healing I perform, and every meal I break with others. Love transcends boundaries and speaks to the deepest longings of the human heart. It is the radical, transformative power that has the ability to heal wounds and restore hope. In my ministry, I will embody this love, inviting others to experience its depth and breadth.

In this sacred space of reflection, I turn my thoughts to prayer. I close my eyes and center myself, seeking guidance and strength for the path that lies ahead. "Father," I whisper, "I am here, ready to embrace the journey you have laid before me. Grant me the wisdom to lead with compassion and the courage to stand firm in the face of adversity. May my heart remain open to those who seek refuge, and may I be a vessel for your love in the world."

I ask for clarity in my teachings, that they may resonate deeply with those who hear them. I seek strength for the moments of doubt that may arise, so I can remain steadfast in my purpose. Above all, I pray for the community that surrounds me, that together we may become a beacon of hope for those in darkness.

As I finish my prayer, I feel a deep sense of peace wash over me. The uncertainties of the future no longer feel overwhelming; instead, they are invitations to grow and learn. I know that each challenge will serve to deepen my understanding of love and grace.

With renewed resolve, I open my eyes to the horizon. The journey of ministry awaits, filled with potential and promise. I stand ready to embrace the unfolding story, to share my heart with the world, and to reflect the love that has been bestowed upon me. The path will be demanding, but I am committed to walking it with faith, guided by the community I cherish and the love that drives me forward.

And so, with a heart full of hope and determination, I take my first step into the unknown, ready to embrace the beautiful, transformative journey that lies ahead.

Golgotha awaits.

Chapter 4: The Miracles and Teachings

As I reflect on my ministry, I am reminded that the miracles I performed were not merely extraordinary events; they were powerful expressions of God's love and authority. Each miracle unfolded in a unique context, surrounded by the hopes and fears of the people who witnessed them. They were moments where heaven touched earth, where the impossible became possible, and where faith was ignited in the hearts of those who saw.

In the dusty streets of Galilee, amidst the whispers of doubt and the weight of despair, I stepped into a world longing for healing and hope. The miracles became a focal point of my ministry, a way to reveal the nature of the Kingdom of God. Through these acts, I sought to demonstrate that God's reign was not confined to religious rituals or distant laws but was present in the here and now, actively engaging with humanity.

When I healed the sick, I was not just restoring health; I was proclaiming that the Creator cares deeply for each individual. Every touch, every word of healing was a declaration that the Kingdom of God is marked by compassion and mercy. These acts were signs, tangible manifestations of divine authority that drew people closer, igniting their faith and inspiring them to see the world through a new lens.

The significance of these miracles lies not only in their astonishing nature but in their purpose. Each miracle invited those who witnessed it to consider a deeper reality—one where love triumphs over despair, and hope dispels darkness. When I fed the 5,000, it was more than a display of abundance; it was an invitation to trust in God's provision and to share that abundance with others. It demonstrated that in the Kingdom, everyone is valued, and no one is left hungry or alone.

Miracles were meant to illustrate the heart of the Father, a reflection of His character. They were a call to faith, urging those who witnessed them to recognize the divine presence in their midst. I wanted people to understand that the miracles were not merely for spectacle but were invitations to enter into a relationship with God—a relationship built on trust, love, and a recognition of His power in our lives.

As I journeyed through towns and villages, I encountered many who were desperate for a miracle, and in those moments, I saw the profound impact that hope could have. When someone believed that healing was possible, when they dared to hope for a better tomorrow, that faith opened the door for miracles to unfold. It was a reminder to me that faith, even as small as a mustard seed, holds the power to move mountains.

In performing these miracles, I also sought to challenge the social and religious norms of my time. I reached out to the marginalized—the lepers, the blind, the outcasts—showing that in God's eyes, no one is beyond redemption or care. Each act of healing was a statement against the barriers that society had erected, illustrating that the Kingdom of God transcends boundaries of culture, class, and convention.

As I reflect on the miracles, I see them as an integral part of my mission—a mission rooted in love and compassion. They were expressions of divine authority that called people to a new understanding of God's heart and His desire for restoration. These moments were pivotal not only for those who experienced them but also for the burgeoning community of followers who witnessed the power of faith in action.

These miracles served as both a gift and a challenge. They were gifts of grace to those who received them, but they also challenged each observer to respond with their own faith. Each miracle was a reflection of the Kingdom—an invitation to experience God's love firsthand and to participate in the transformative work that was unfolding. As I continue to walk this path, I am reminded that every act of love, every healing touch, and every shared meal is a reflection of the divine purpose that drives my ministry and the deep, abiding call to live out the values of the Kingdom of God.

Pain radiates through me, my shoulders numb from the weight of the cross. I waver, stumbling slightly, yet in this moment of uncertainty, I pause to reflect on the love and sacrifice that define my path.

As I recall the day of the feeding of the 5,000, I can still feel the energy of that moment, the anticipation in the air. The sun was beginning to dip low in the sky, casting a warm glow over the vast crowd that had gathered on the grassy hillside. People from all walks of life had come to hear my teachings, drawn by the hope that perhaps they might find answers to their deepest questions or healing for their troubled hearts. Their faces were a tapestry of emotions—curiosity, longing, and, above all, hunger.

The disciples were bustling around me, their faces a mix of excitement and anxiety as they took in the magnitude of the gathering. "Master, send the people away," they urged, concern etched on their brows. "It's getting late, and there's nowhere for them to eat." They worried about the practicalities, the logistics of feeding such a vast multitude in a remote place. I sensed their doubt, the gnawing worry that overshadowed their faith. They had witnessed miracles, yet in that moment, their vision was clouded by the impossibility of the task before us.

Looking out over the crowd, my heart swelled with compassion. These were not just faces; they were souls, each with their own stories, their own struggles. I could see the weariness in their eyes, the physical fatigue that came from a long day of listening and learning. "They do not need to go away," I told my disciples. "You give them something to eat."

With that simple statement, I aimed to shift their perspective. I wanted them to recognize that within the constraints of our reality lay the seeds of divine possibility. But my words only deepened their concerns. "We have only five loaves of bread and two fish," they responded, their voices tinged with frustration. It was a paltry offering, insufficient for the task at hand.

In that moment, I took the loaves and the fish, lifting them to heaven in a gesture of gratitude. I knew that the act of giving thanks was crucial. It was a reminder to myself and to those around me that abundance is born from gratitude, and that all good things come from the Father. As I broke the bread, I sensed the shift in the atmosphere—the miracle was beginning.

As I distributed the food to the disciples, I felt an overwhelming sense of joy and excitement coursing through me. With each piece that passed through my hands, the food multiplied, defying logic and expectation. The disciples began to serve the crowd, their initial doubts replaced by awe as they witnessed the miraculous transformation of those meager resources into a feast. Laughter and joy rippled through the people as they realized they would not leave hungry.

I watched as the crowd, once anxious and tired, began to eat and share with one another, their faces lighting up with joy. The sound of their laughter and the crunch of bread filled the air, a beautiful symphony of gratitude and fellowship. In that moment, I understood that the miracle was not just about filling stomachs; it was a profound demonstration of how sharing leads to abundance.

When all had eaten and were satisfied, I instructed my disciples to gather the leftovers. To their astonishment, they filled twelve baskets with what remained. This excess spoke volumes about the generosity of God. It was a powerful reminder that when we share what we have, no matter how small, God multiplies it in ways we cannot fathom. The miracle was a testament to trust—trust in God's provision and the necessity of community in meeting the needs of others.

As I reflected on this experience, I realized that it encapsulated a key aspect of my ministry. The feeding of the 5,000 was about much more than just physical nourishment; it was a lesson in faith, community, and divine abundance. I wanted those gathered to see that when we come together, sharing our resources and our love, we participate in the work of God's Kingdom.

In our everyday lives, we often find ourselves overwhelmed by the enormity of the needs around us. It's easy to feel like our contributions are insignificant in the face of such challenges. Yet, this miracle teaches us that even the smallest act of generosity can create ripples of change. When we offer what we have—whether it's food, time, or love—God can transform it into something extraordinary.

I want those who hear this story to remember that God provides for His people, often in ways we do not expect. The feeding of the 5,000 reminds us that divine provision is not just about meeting physical needs; it encompasses emotional and spiritual nourishment as well. When we open our hearts to one another and trust in God's ability to multiply our efforts, we become vessels of His grace, reflecting the very essence of the Kingdom.

The lesson is clear: in community, we find strength; in sharing, we experience abundance; and in faith, we discover the boundless possibilities that God offers. As I stumble toward Golgotha, I carry these lessons close to my heart, knowing they will guide those who follow in my footsteps.

The crowd left that day not only with full stomachs but with full hearts—reminded that they are part of something greater, a family bound together by love, faith, and the miraculous provision of God. And as they walked away, I smiled, knowing that this was but one of many lessons I would share along the way.

I lose my footing under the weight of the cross, each breath a struggle. I pause, heart heavy, reflecting inwardly on love, sacrifice, and the pain that leads to redemption

As I walk through the towns and villages, the cries of those in need often reach my ears before I see them. Each person—each story—carries a weight of suffering that tugs at my heart. The blind man sitting by the roadside, the leper shunned from society, the paralyzed man longing for connection—these are not mere encounters; they are moments that define the essence of my mission.

I remember one particular day when the sun hung low in the sky, casting a warm golden hue over the land. A crowd had gathered, drawn by the hope of healing. Among them was a blind man, his sight stolen by darkness. As I approached, I felt the weight of his despair. His hand outstretched, trembling with uncertainty. I knelt beside him, asking gently what he desired.

"Rabbi, I want to see," he whispered, his voice filled with longing.

In that moment, I placed my hands on his eyes and prayed, feeling the surge of divine energy coursing through me. "Receive your sight; your faith has healed you." As my hands fell away, I witnessed the astonishment on his face, a transformation from darkness to light. He opened his eyes, and tears streamed down his cheeks as he gazed upon the world for the first time.

The crowd erupted in joy, their amazement palpable. This miracle was not just an act of healing; it was a reminder of hope—an affirmation that no one is beyond the reach of compassion.

In another encounter, I met a leper, a man pushed to the fringes of society, isolated from family and friends. His body bore the scars of his affliction, and his eyes reflected years of loneliness. The law dictated that he should remain unclean, shunned by all. But as I approached, he fell to his knees, desperation etched on his face.

"Lord, if you are willing, you can make me clean," he cried.

Moved with compassion, I reached out and touched him—an act that broke societal norms. "I am willing; be clean!" The leprosy vanished instantly, and for the first time in years, he felt the warmth of human touch. It was not just healing of the body; it was a restoration of his humanity.

I always seek to connect with those I heal. Each miracle is infused with love, a personal touch that bridges the gap between the divine and the suffering. Moments of prayer are my lifeline, grounding me in the presence of the Father as I minister to those in need.

Healing is more than alleviating physical suffering; it is about restoring dignity and faith. Each encounter allows me to glimpse the profound impact of compassion. When the paralyzed man was lowered through the roof by his friends, their determination resonated with me. I could see the love they had for him, the lengths they were willing to go to bring him to me.

"Take heart, son; your sins are forgiven," I said, and then to the crowd, "Which is easier to say: your sins are forgiven, or to say, 'Get up and walk'? But I want you to know that the Son of Man has authority on earth to forgive sins." I turned to the man and commanded, "Get up, take your mat, and go home." In that moment, the entire room was transformed—not just by the miracle but by the realization of what it means to be truly restored.

The call to serve others is woven into the fabric of these miracles. Each healing is a testament to the power of love in action. I often remind those around me that it is not just my touch that heals; it is their faith that opens the door to transformation. Each act of kindness, every moment of connection, has the potential to restore hope and dignity to those who feel lost.

As I reflect on these miracles, I understand that they are not solely about the miraculous acts themselves but about the love that drives them. Each healing encourages us to embrace our role as servants, to extend compassion and grace to those around us. This journey is not just mine; it is ours—a shared mission to bring light into the darkness, to heal the broken-hearted, and to invite all into the embrace of community.

Agonizing pain courses through my body, my neck and shoulders feel heavy and numb beneath the crushing weight of the cross. I waver, my steps faltering, but in this raw moment of uncertainty, I pause to immerse myself in the profound love and sacrifice that shape my journey.

As I reflect on these miracles, the lessons they impart resonate deeply within me. Each healing moment is a tapestry woven with threads of compassion, faith, and community, showcasing the very essence of my mission.

Returning to the blind man, I recall how his joy became a catalyst for others. After regaining his sight, he couldn't contain his excitement. He began to proclaim what had happened, drawing more people to witness the power of faith. This ripple effect is vital; it reminds us that our experiences of healing can inspire hope in others. Each miracle I perform is not just a singular event; it is an invitation for the community to believe in the possibility of transformation. The leper's story is etched in my heart, not only for the miracle itself but for the societal implications it carries. After I healed him, he rushed back to his family and friends, breaking the chains of isolation. His return symbolized more than physical healing; it was a reclamation of his life and identity. In that moment, he became a testament to the love and acceptance that transcends societal barriers.

I think of how crucial it is for us to acknowledge the outcasts, the ones society deems unworthy. In every healing, I strive to show that love knows no boundaries. It invites the marginalized back into the fold, creating a community that thrives on acceptance and compassion.

The paralyzed man's story also illustrates the profound power of community. His friends' determination to bring him to me, even at the cost of disrupting a gathering, speaks volumes about the bonds of love and support we must cultivate. They exemplified what it means to carry one another's burdens, reminding me that healing is often a communal effort.

When he stood up, rolled up his mat, and walked home, the atmosphere was electric. The crowd witnessed not only a physical miracle but a deep spiritual awakening. They began to understand that faith and healing are intertwined; that sometimes, it is the faith of others that carries us through our darkest moments.

These miracles serve as a microcosm of the greater message I seek to impart: that God's love is expansive and available to all, regardless of their circumstances. Through each act of healing, I endeavor to reveal the Kingdom of God—a realm where love prevails, hope reigns, and every soul is valued.

Every time I extend my hand to heal, I am reminding the world that the divine is present in the mundane, that moments of grace can transform lives. The purpose behind these miracles is to illustrate that faith can bridge gaps, restore relationships, and rekindle the human spirit.

As I ponder the significance of these events, I also feel a call to action for those who witness these miracles. Each individual has a role to play in this divine narrative. My teachings emphasize that healing can take many forms—sometimes, it is a kind word, a listening ear, or a simple act of service. The stories of the blind man, the leper, and the paralyzed man remind us that we are all called to be conduits of healing in our communities. In recognizing the struggles of others, we can offer support and love, helping to restore dignity and hope.

These experiences shape my understanding of compassion and service. The miracles are not mere spectacles; they are invitations for all of humanity to embrace love in action. Each healed person becomes a beacon of hope, demonstrating that faith is powerful enough to overcome any obstacle.

As I move forward in my ministry, I carry these reflections with me. They ground me in my purpose and remind me of the profound impact we can have when we embody love and compassion. In every interaction, I strive to be a source of light, healing not just bodies but hearts and souls, urging each person to recognize their worth in the eyes of God.

I fall, the ground rushing up to meet me, a moment of vulnerability that echoes my pain. As I struggle to rise, memories flood back—faces of those I've loved, moments of joy and sorrow, reminding me of the strength and hope that carry me forward.

I strain to stand.

Breathe

I walked through the bustling streets of Capernaum, I was approached by a Roman centurion, a man of authority and power. His servant was gravely ill, and the centurion, despite his position, was desperate for help. He understood the complexities of faith, recognizing that true power lies not in control but in humility.

"Lord," he said, "I do not deserve to have you come under my roof. But just say the word, and my servant will be healed." His faith astounded me. Here was a man accustomed to commanding respect, yet he humbly sought my help, trusting in my authority to heal from a distance.

I marveled at his belief. "Go; let it be done just as you believed it would," I replied. At that very hour, his servant was healed. This miracle emphasized that faith knows no boundaries, transcending social hierarchies and cultural barriers. It illustrated the Kingdom of God, where belief and trust can bring about transformation, regardless of one's status.

I push against the weight

Breathe

I remember healing a woman who had suffered from bleeding for twelve years. She approached me timidly in a crowd, believing that if she could just touch the hem of my garment, she would be healed.

As she reached out, I felt power leave me. "Who touched me?" I asked, sensing her faith.

When she revealed herself, trembling with fear and hope, I said, "Daughter, your faith has healed you. Go in peace and be freed from your suffering." It was a moment that exemplified the importance of faith and the profound restoration of not just health but also identity.

Muscles quiver.

Breathe

The winds howled like a fierce beast, tossing our small boat upon the churning waters of the Sea of Galilee. The sky darkened, and waves crashed over the sides, drenching us with icy spray. I could see the fear etched on the faces of my disciples, men who were seasoned fishermen yet now felt powerless against the tempest.

"Master, we're going to drown!" they cried, voices filled with panic as they struggled to keep the boat afloat. Their fear was palpable, a storm of its own, intensifying with every crashing wave.

I remained in the stern, resting, seemingly undisturbed by the chaos around us. My heart, however, was full of compassion for my friends. I knew their fear came not just from the storm but from a deeper uncertainty—an uncertainty about their own safety and their place in this unfolding story.

Every breath is a battle.

Breathe

As the boat pitched violently, I stood and faced the storm. The wind howled, but my voice rang out with authority, "Peace! Be still!" Instantly, the winds ceased, and the waves settled into a serene calm. It was as if creation itself recognized the voice of its Creator.

The disciples stared in disbelief, their fear shifting to awe. "Who is this?" they whispered among themselves. "Even the wind and the waves obey him!"

In that moment, I felt a profound connection to the power of faith. The storm outside was nothing compared to the storms that raged within the hearts of my disciples. My words were not just for the winds; they were an invitation for my followers to trust in my presence, even when the seas of life become tumultuous.

Pain fuels my resolve.

Breathe

This miracle was not merely about calming the physical storm but about addressing the storms within each of us. Life is fraught with uncertainties—loss, fear, and doubt. I knew that my disciples would face trials and tribulations in the days to come, and I wanted them to understand the importance of faith amidst chaos.

As I gazed at the still waters, I reflected on how often we allow fear to dictate our reactions. Just as the waves can be fierce and overwhelming, so too can life's challenges. Yet, it is in these moments that we must remember that we are never truly alone. My presence, like the calm after the storm, brings peace even when circumstances seem dire.

The lesson of the storm was clear: trust. Trust in the unseen, trust in the divine plan that transcends our understanding. Just as I commanded the winds, so too can we find the strength to command our fears through faith.

Trust in my presence, for I am with you always, even in the darkest of nights. In every storm, there lies an opportunity for growth, a chance to deepen your faith, and a reminder of the peace that surpasses all understanding. So, as you navigate the storms of your own life, hold fast to that faith, and you will find the calm within the chaos.

I refuse to stay down.

Breathe

I rise, trembling.

Breathe

Determination ignites.

I steady myself.

I steady myself, gathering what little strength remains, and slowly open my eyes, letting the world come into focus again, aware of both the pain and the light that surrounds me. I reflect.

As I walked among the people, sharing the message of love, compassion, and the Kingdom of God, I often chose to teach through parables—simple stories that carried profound truths. Why parables? Because they invite listeners into the narrative, allowing them to find themselves within the tale. A well-told story captures the imagination and stirs the heart, making complex spiritual truths accessible and relatable.

Each parable serves as a mirror, reflecting the realities of life and faith. They are not merely lessons to be learned but invitations to enter a deeper understanding of God's character and the values of His Kingdom. Through these stories, I sought to provoke thought, inspire action, and illuminate the path to a fuller life rooted in love.

One of my most cherished parables is that of the Good Samaritan: a man traveling from Jerusalem to Jericho fell among thieves. They stripped him, beat him, and left him half dead. As he lay there, both a priest and a Levite passed by without offering help. But then came a Samaritan—a group often despised by many—who saw the wounded man and was moved with compassion.

He tended to his wounds, carried him to an inn, and paid for his care. Through this story, I illustrated the essence of loving one's neighbor, transcending cultural and social boundaries. True compassion knows no limits; it does not ask who is worthy but seeks to serve those in need.

One small step.

Another powerful story I shared is that of the Prodigal Son; here a younger son asks for his inheritance early, squanders it in reckless living, and eventually finds himself destitute. In his despair, he decides to return home, expecting rejection. Instead, his father runs to him, embraces him, and celebrates his return with a feast. This parable beautifully captures the nature of forgiveness and unconditional love. It speaks to those who feel lost or unworthy, reminding them that no matter how far one strays, the Father's love is always ready to receive them. It emphasizes the joy of reconciliation and the transformative power of love that knows no bounds.

Another small step.

In the parable of the Sower, I described a farmer scattering seeds, some falling on the path, some on rocky ground, some among thorns, and some on good soil. The seeds represent the Word of God, and the varying outcomes illustrate how people respond to that message. This parable invites introspection about our receptivity to God's teachings. Are we open and nurturing like good soil, or do we allow distractions and difficulties to choke our spiritual growth? It highlights the importance of cultivating a heart that is willing to receive and respond to the divine message, emphasizing that everyone has the potential to bear fruit.

As I stagger slowly along the road to Golgotha, each step heavy with pain and purpose, I catch a glimpse of a woman pushing through the crowd; her gaze filled with compassion and understanding.

I feel the warmth of her presence as she draws closer, her heart reaching out to me amidst the jeers and shouts. In a moment of grace, she steps forward and gently wipes my face with her veil, her touch soft and tender against my bruised skin.

In that brief encounter, I sense her empathy, her willingness to alleviate my suffering, even if just for a moment. Her act, so simple yet profound, reminds me of the love I carry for all humanity. I am grateful, knowing that even in my darkest hour, there are souls willing to share in my pain, to offer solace.

As she pulls away, I see the streaks of my blood and sweat on her cloth, a symbol of the shared burden we all carry. With a flicker of hope ignited in my heart, I continue my journey, knowing that love persists even in the face of despair.

As I continued to gather followers, I witnessed both fervent devotion and hesitance. Some stepped forward boldly, eyes bright with hope and anticipation, while others lingered in the shadows, contemplating the weight of their decision. I remembered the early days of my own ministry—how thrilling yet intimidating it felt to respond to my calling. I encouraged my followers to reflect on their motivations and desires.

In moments of prayer and conversation, I emphasized the importance of perseverance in the face of adversity. "In this world, you will have trouble," I reminded them, yet I also reassured them, "Take heart! I have overcome the world." This was not a journey to be undertaken lightly, but with the understanding that the rewards of faith and community far outweighed the challenges.

Many of my followers would face trials—misunderstanding from family, persecution from the authorities, and the heavy burden of carrying my message into a world that often rejected it. I sought to instill in them a sense of purpose and commitment that would sustain them through difficulties. Together, we prayed for strength, guidance, and an unwavering spirit to press on.

Chapter 5: The Disciples

As I walk towards Golgotha, I scan the faces in the crowd, feeling the weight of their stares—some filled with scorn, others with sorrow. In the midst of this turmoil, I hope to catch sight of my disciples, the ones I have walked with, taught, and loved deeply.

But as I struggle forward, my heart sinks; most have fled in fear, unable to bear witness to this agony. I catch glimpses of a few familiar faces—Peter, trembling and distraught, trying to blend into the shadows; John, his eyes filled with tears, standing resolutely despite the danger.

Their presence, though distant, stirs something within me—a bittersweet reminder of our shared moments of joy and teaching. In this darkest hour, their love gives me strength, even as they grapple with their own fears. I long to comfort them, to tell them that this suffering has meaning, that through it all, love will prevail.

Yet, as I take another painful step, I realize that I must face this journey alone, carrying not just my cross but the weight of their hopes and fears as well.

The pain I bear is intertwined with beautiful memories that both comfort and wound me. I recall the laughter shared with my disciples, the warmth of their companionship, and the moments of profound revelation. Each memory brings an inner smile, yet it cuts deep, reminding me of the fleeting nature of joy. The love we shared now feels like a distant echo against the backdrop of my suffering. These cherished moments become bittersweet, their beauty amplified by the impending loss. In this journey of agony, I carry their essence within me, a haunting reminder of all that I hold dear.

The weight of the cross on my shoulders brings back a flood of memories—memories of those who walked beside me in the days of my ministry. The dust beneath my feet seems to whisper their names: Peter, James,

John, Matthew, and the others who answered my call with both courage and hesitation.

In a world burdened by Roman rule and the weight of tradition, I found a ragtag group of individuals, each longing for purpose. I remember the fervent energy of our gatherings, the laughter echoing under the olive trees, and the quiet moments of reflection as we shared meals and teachings. Discipleship is more than a title; it's a profound relationship built on trust, learning, and shared experiences.

I invited fishermen from the shores of Galilee and a tax collector from a bustling town, knowing that my call would turn their lives upside down. They came with their own dreams, insecurities, and expectations. Each one carried a story that shaped them, just as my presence began to shape their futures.

As I think of Peter, I recall his bold spirit—always ready to speak up, sometimes before he thought it through. His heart was loyal, even when doubt crept in. Then there were the brothers, James and John, with their fiery ambition and dreams of greatness. I see Matthew, once a symbol of betrayal as a tax collector, now transformed into a beacon of grace.

With each of them, I wove lessons of love, humility, and forgiveness into our shared journey. There were moments of joy, where we celebrated the miracles and the people we healed, and moments of struggle, where I had to remind them of the power of faith amidst their doubts.

As I stumble forward, I remember the lessons I imparted—how to love unconditionally, how to serve others, and how to embrace humility. These teachings were not just for their own growth but for the greater mission we shared, one that would continue even after I was gone.

Now, as I approach my destiny, I carry each of them in my heart, knowing that the foundation we built together will echo through the ages.

My thoughts drift to Peter—the rock I leaned on in moments of doubt, and the one who stumbled when I needed him most.

I can still see the scene by the Sea of Galilee, the sun glinting off the water. It was a day like any other for Peter, worn from fishing all night with no catch to show for his efforts. When I asked him to let down his nets again, I saw the flicker of skepticism in his eyes. "Master, we've worked hard all night and haven't caught anything," he said, but still, he did as I asked. And when those nets filled to bursting, I witnessed a transformation in him—a glimpse of the man he could become. He fell to his knees, overwhelmed, saying, "Go away from me, Lord; I am a sinful man." In that moment, I understood that his heart was both humble and hungry for something greater.

Peter was the one who stepped out boldly, declaring me the Messiah. His conviction was a flame that ignited the hearts of many. Yet, he was also the one who faltered, and I can't shake the ache of that night in the garden. As I was taken away, I watched him follow at a distance, his face shadowed by fear. When the servant girl challenged him, "You also were with Jesus," I felt the piercing sorrow of his denial. Three times he denied me, and each time it felt like a dagger to my heart. I remember the rooster crowing, marking the moment of his failure—how he broke down, weeping, realizing what he had done.

It was a heavy burden to bear, knowing that my closest friend had turned away in my hour of need. But even then, my love for him never wavered. After my resurrection, I sought him out, knowing he needed to hear my voice. I found him by the shore, casting his nets into the water, lost in despair. I called to him, and when he recognized me, he leapt from the boat and swam to me.

"Do you love me?" I asked him three times, a question not just about affection, but about his very purpose. Each time he answered, "Yes, Lord," I could see the burden lift from his shoulders, the shame dissolve into the salty air. I told him, "Feed my sheep," reminding him that even in his failure, he was called to serve, to lead, to love.

Peter taught me about the rawness of humanity—the mix of courage and cowardice, the dance of faith and doubt. He showed me that true loyalty doesn't mean perfection; it means coming back, even after stumbling. Through him, I learned the power of forgiveness, the grace that can transform the broken-hearted into pillars of strength.

As I walk toward Golgotha, I hold Peter close in my heart. He is a reflection of my own journey—one marked by moments of profound connection and painful separation. I pray he remembers that even in his darkest hour, he is loved and never truly lost. My hope is that he will carry the lessons of our time together, sharing the message of grace and redemption with the world.

Peter, my rock, my friend—though I am leaving this earth, the bond we forged will endure. In his heart, I see the flickering flame of faith, ready to ignite the world.

I feel the heat of the tears in my eyes, a mix of anguish and longing that threatens to spill over. Each tear is a testament to the weight of my heart, reflecting the pain I carry—not for myself, but for Peter. In this moment, I am acutely aware of his love for me, intertwined with sorrow and hope. I blink, trying to steady myself, yet the emotion wells up within me, urging me to embrace this vulnerability. It is a profound reminder that even in the depths of despair, love remains a powerful force, guiding me forward on this difficult path.

My thoughts turn to two of my dearest companions—James and John, the Sons of Thunder. Their fiery spirits and unyielding loyalty have always inspired me, and in these final moments, I reflect on our journey together and the lessons we learned along the way.

I remember the day I first called them. They were mending their nets by the Sea of Galilee, just like Peter. The energy between us was electric, an immediate bond forged by a shared purpose. "Follow me," I said, and without hesitation, they left their father and their livelihood behind. It was an act of faith, a leap into the unknown, and I could see the eagerness in their eyes, the promise of adventure ahead. They were passionate and impulsive, often quick to react—traits that would serve them well and challenge them deeply.

But their ambition sometimes overshadowed their understanding. I recall the day they came to me, their eyes gleaming with a mix of hope and bravado. "Grant us to sit, one at your right hand and one at your left, in your glory," they requested, a bold appeal for positions of honor. I looked into their faces, seeing the fire of their desire but also the misunderstanding of true greatness. "You do not know what you are asking," I replied, reminding them that the path ahead was one of suffering and servanthood. It was a moment that defined them—a testament to their yearning for significance, yet a stark reminder of the lessons yet to be learned.

Over time, I watched as their ambition transformed. The fiery passion that once sought personal glory began to shift toward a deeper understanding of service and sacrifice. They witnessed my humility as I washed their feet, and in those intimate moments, the truth of leadership became clear: it is found in love, not in titles. They learned that the Kingdom of God is not about power, but about lifting others up.

James and John shared many defining moments with me—the Transfiguration on the mountain, where they glimpsed my divine glory and felt the weight of their calling. They saw the light that radiated from me, yet I knew that even that glimpse was just the beginning of their journey toward true understanding. It was in those moments of divine revelation that they began to grasp the profound nature of sacrifice and service.

As I walk now, preparing for my earthly end, my heart swells with love for them. I think of the resilience they will need when I am gone. The early church will rely on their strength, their passion, and their commitment to love one another as I loved them. I hope they remember that the essence of our time together was not in seeking honor but in serving each other and those in need.

Their journey will not be easy. The weight of leadership, the struggle against their own ambitions—it will challenge them in ways they cannot yet imagine. But I have faith in them. I have seen their hearts soften and grow. I know that they will become pillars of the early church, embodying the teachings of love and servanthood that I have imparted to them.

In these final moments, as I reflect on James and John, I am filled with hope. They are not just my disciples; they are my brothers. Together, we have walked through the fire of doubt and emerged stronger. I pray that they will continue to embrace the cost of discipleship, holding on to the truth that greatness lies in love and service.

As I approach the culmination of my journey, I carry them with me in spirit, knowing that their hearts are forever changed. The Sons of Thunder will become messengers of peace, and in their hands, they will carry the flame of love into the world.

As I struggle forward, an inner strength begins to rise within me, fueled by memories of James and John. Their laughter, their unwavering faith, and the way they stood by me through trials spark a warmth in my heart. I remember the moments we shared—the lessons taught, the love exchanged. Despite the pain coursing through my body, their spirit instills a renewed sense of purpose in me.

I envision their faces, filled with determination, their eyes reflecting the commitment they showed as my closest friends. It is as if their presence lifts me, reminding me that this journey is not solely for my own sake but for the hope and salvation of all humanity. In their memory, I find a reservoir of courage, a reminder that love and faith can transcend even the darkest of hours. With each step, I carry their essence, drawing strength from our bond as I continue toward my destiny.

My mind drifts to Matthew, the tax collector—an unexpected choice among my disciples. His story is one of profound transformation, a testament to the boundless grace that defines our mission.

I remember the moment I called him. He was sitting at his booth, collecting taxes, a position that branded him an outsider in our community. The disdain of the people was palpable; he was often seen as a traitor, a thief in their eyes. But when I approached him, something shifted. "Follow me," I said simply, and without hesitation, he left everything behind—his booth, his wealth, his past. It was a remarkable leap of faith, one that demonstrated the power of my call to transform even the most marginalized.

Matthew's journey with us was marked by moments of incredible growth. As a former tax collector, he offered a unique perspective that enriched our ministry. He understood the struggles of those on the fringes of society, having been one of them. His experiences lent depth to our discussions and a sense of empathy that resonated with others. I could see him gradually shedding the weight of his past, embracing the freedom that came with acceptance and love.

Through Matthew, I taught the significance of grace. He understood, perhaps better than any of us, that everyone is worthy of redemption, no matter their past. He often reminded us that those who are well do not need a physician, but those who are sick do. "I desire mercy, not sacrifice," I had told him, emphasizing that my mission was to seek the lost and embrace the broken-hearted.

Matthew's unique insights and commitment to sharing the good news would later lead him to write the Gospel that bears his name, offering a profound witness to the life and teachings of our time together. He became a bridge for many who felt unworthy, demonstrating that no one is beyond the reach of God's love.

As I reflect on Matthew's transformation, I am filled with gratitude. His journey reminds me of the essence of our ministry—that grace knows no boundaries, that acceptance is powerful, and that every heart can be changed by love. In these final moments, I hold his story close, knowing that he will continue to inspire others to seek and embrace the truth of God's mercy long after I am gone.

Matthew stands as a powerful testament to the truth that people from all walks of life can embrace my teachings. Once a tax collector, often despised and marginalized, he chose to follow his heart. His transformation is a reminder that no one is beyond redemption, and that every soul can open to love and grace. Matthew's journey inspires me to look beyond societal labels and judgments. His faith and dedication show us all that true discipleship is rooted in the willingness to change and to serve others. In his story, I see hope for not just the lost and the broken, but as a light that encourages all to seek a deeper connection with the divine. Through Matthew, we learn that it is never too late to embrace a path of love, compassion, and purpose, inviting everyone to walk in the light of my teachings.

My mind turns to Andrew, Peter's brother, with his quiet but determined spirit. It was he who first introduced Peter to me, a simple act that would change the course of many lives. Andrew had an innate ability to connect others with the truth. I see him standing by the shores of the Sea of Galilee, eager to share the good news. His heart was always open to others, drawing people in with his genuine nature. He recognized the potential in others before they even saw it in themselves, a true servant of the Kingdom.

Then there was Philip, a seeker of truth who often voiced the questions others were afraid to ask. I remember one instance when he approached me with uncertainty, saying, "Lord, show us the Father, and that will be enough for us." His desire to understand was palpable. It reminded me that doubt can be a pathway to deeper faith. Philip's questions pushed us all to explore the depths of our beliefs, to seek answers and challenge assumptions. I admired his courage to voice his uncertainties, knowing that such honesty is vital for growth.

And how could I forget Nathanael? His skepticism was sharp, yet it was in that very skepticism that I saw his strength. When I first called him, he expressed doubt, questioning how anything good could come from Nazareth. But when he came to see for himself, he was transformed. "Rabbi, you are the Son of God; you are the king of Israel!" he exclaimed upon realizing the truth. Nathanael's journey from skepticism to faith mirrored so many others, a reminder that doubts can lead to deeper understanding.

Then there was Judas, a name that carries heavy weight in my heart. He began as one of my closest followers, displaying the loyalty and dedication that I valued so much. Yet, beneath the surface, a darkness grew. I recall the moment at the Last Supper when I revealed that one of my own would betray me. The anguish in Judas's eyes as he accepted the morsel I offered was a mix of loyalty and impending betrayal. I wish I could have reached him, pulled him back from the edge. His journey serves as a poignant reminder of the fragility of the human heart—the capacity for both loyalty and failure.

As I pressed on, a soldiers' fist echoed in my ears, mingling with the sounds of the crowd. Each hit felt like a betrayal, yet I reminded myself of the greater purpose behind this suffering. I chose to respond to the soldiers' violence with silent grace, embodying the love I preached. Even in this darkest hour, I held onto the belief that forgiveness could break through the hardest hearts. As I continued forward, I felt a quiet determination to transform this pain into something beautiful—a path to redemption for all who would come after me.

My disciples, I see the beauty in our diversity. Each of them brought unique perspectives, strengths, and weaknesses to our mission. Together, we learned the value of community, the importance of embracing one another despite our differences. I taught them that the Kingdom of God flourishes when each person contributes their gifts, whether it be through connection, questioning, skepticism, or even betrayal.

In these final moments, I carry the weight of their stories with me. They each have lessons to share—of faith, love, and the journey of understanding. I hope they remember that even amidst pain and failure, there is always the potential for redemption. My heart swells with gratitude for the time we shared, knowing that they will carry the lessons of compassion, acceptance, and hope into the world.

As I walk this path toward crucifixion, my heart is heavy, yet I find solace in the thought of what lies ahead for them. I hold a profound hope for my disciples. Their role as messengers of my love and teachings will extend far beyond our time together. They will carry the flame of faith into the world, inspiring others to embrace the transformative power of love and service.

As I stagger forward, I am filled with gratitude for the relationships we forged. Each disciple has left an indelible mark on my heart, and I trust that they will continue to embody the values we cherished together. Their legacy will be a testament to the enduring impact of discipleship, encouraging future generations to live out their faith with courage, compassion, and unwavering dedication.

In the end, it is love that will bind us all, transcending time and space, inviting everyone to partake in the beautiful, transformative journey of faith.

Chapter 6: Moments of Doubt and Strength

As I carry the cross, I feel the rough splinters digging into my shoulders, each jagged edge a sharp reminder of my burden. The wood bites into my skin, sending waves of pain radiating through my body. With every small step, the pressure intensifies, a cruel juxtaposition to the love I hold within. Each splinter is a testament to the weight of humanity's sins, digging deeper with every falter. Yet, in this agony, I find purpose; this pain is a part of the sacrifice I willingly embrace. It fuels my resolve, reminding me that through suffering, hope and redemption can emerge.

Through my pain I find myself reflecting on the profound, often hidden, struggle of doubt. It is a feeling that courses through the veins of every human being, a shadow that dances alongside the light of faith. In these moments of impending sacrifice, I recognize that doubt is not the absence of faith, but rather a part of the human experience—a testament to our vulnerability and our yearning for something greater.

Throughout my ministry, I have encountered doubt in many forms: from my disciples grappling with their own fears, to the crowds who would waver in their belief, swayed by the winds of opinion. They are not alone in their struggles; I too have felt the tremors of uncertainty shake the very foundation of my resolve. The expectations placed upon me were immense—soaring high like the mountains, often leaving me to wonder if I could truly fulfill the role that had been set before me.

In the quiet moments of reflection, when the hustle of the world falls away, I have wrestled with my purpose. The weight of my mission, the impending crucifixion, has often left me feeling small and overwhelmed. Yet, it is in these moments of doubt that I have found clarity and strength. I have learned that acknowledging my fears does not diminish my call; rather, it deepens my understanding of what it means to be human. My vulnerabilities remind me of my connection to those I have come to serve, those who look to me for hope and healing.

In this, the honest reflections of my struggles. I reflect on not only the doubts that have haunted me, but also the moments of strength that have emerged in their wake. Leadership is often perceived as a steadfastness unmarred by uncertainty, but I have come to understand that true leadership embraces vulnerability. It is in the willingness to show our authentic selves that we foster deeper connections with others.

As I recount these moments—both fraught with fear and illuminated by strength—I hope to offer a glimpse into the interplay between doubt and resolve. For in embracing our vulnerabilities, we can discover a profound source of power, one that enables us to rise above our fears and lead with compassion and authenticity. In these reflections, may we all find the courage to confront our own doubts and recognize them as integral to our journeys of faith.

As I move forward on this path to Golgotha, the enormity of expectations weighs heavily upon me. From the moment I stepped into my role as inspired teacher, the world began to look at me through a lens of hope and demand. The religious leaders scrutinized my every word and action, eager to find fault. The crowds clamored for miracles and signs, their faith teetering on the edge of desperation. Even my own disciples, who had shared in my journey, carried their own hopes and uncertainties about what it meant to follow me.

I can, now, in this moment, still feel the pressure of those expectations, like a storm pressing in from all sides. They wanted a king, a conqueror who would liberate them from oppression, but I came to bring a different kind of freedom—a freedom from sin, a path to love and redemption. Yet, with each passing day, I felt the weight of their anticipation intensifying. The burden was not just external; it became an internal dialogue, a constant reminder of what I needed to accomplish and the lives resting on my shoulders.

Within this tumultuous sea of expectations, personal fears began to rise. The thought of my impending crucifixion loomed over me like a dark cloud. Would I be able to endure the suffering? Would I fulfill the mission set before me? These questions danced through my mind, often leaving me feeling vulnerable and exposed. The fear of failure gnawed at me, whispering doubts that echoed louder as the time drew closer.

I remember my early days of ministry, filled with enthusiasm and the thrill of connecting with people. But even then, shadows of anxiety would flicker in my heart. Each healing, each teaching, felt like a step further into a destiny I knew would lead to pain. My moments of solitude became increasingly important as I sought clarity and strength. I often withdrew to pray, to find solace, and to wrestle with the weight of my fears in the quiet embrace of the Father.

Now, as I reflect on these fears, I recognize their significance. Acknowledging them did not signify weakness; rather, it became a source of strength. In recognizing my own vulnerability, I found the space to grow. These moments of fear catalyzed a deeper understanding of my mission and helped me connect more profoundly with those around me. It was in my vulnerability that I discovered the essence of empathy—an understanding that transcended mere words and allowed me to walk alongside those who also struggled.

Each time I acknowledged my fears, I felt a release—a reminder that I was not alone in this journey. Just as I faced doubt, so too did those who followed me. This mutual recognition of our humanity forged bonds of understanding and compassion. It allowed me to teach my disciples not just through words, but through the example of grappling with the same emotions that can bind or liberate us.

In the face of fear, I learned to lean into my purpose. Each prayer became a conversation, an invitation for divine strength to fill the spaces where doubt lingered. As I walked this path, I grew to understand that fear could either paralyze or empower. I chose the latter. By embracing my fears, I not only reinforced my own resolve but also prepared my heart to offer comfort to those who would experience their own trials.

In this moment, as I contemplate the journey ahead, I see fear not as an enemy but as a companion that can lead to greater resilience. I hope to impart this lesson to my disciples, to show them that acknowledging their own fears will allow them to grow and ultimately become stronger leaders in their own right. As I continue to move toward my destiny, I carry with me the lessons learned from these moments of fear, ready to embrace whatever lies ahead.

As I stumble my way to Golgotha, I pass near the Garden of Gethsemane, a place rich with memories. Just days before, I had knelt in that garden, praying and wrestling with the weight of what lay ahead. The olive trees stand as silent witnesses to my anguish, the air still heavy with my cries for strength.

Each step I take now feels like a stark contrast to the peace I sought there. The garden symbolizes both my humanity and my divine purpose. As I walk toward my end, I remember the love and support of my disciples, the sorrow I felt for their struggles, and the resolve that grew within me in that sacred place. Though I am surrounded by pain and rejection, the garden remains a poignant reminder of the love that fuels my journey.

I recall the olive trees standing tall and silent, their gnarled branches whispering secrets of time, while the moonlight casts gentle shadows on the path ahead. Usually a place of peace, in this moment it feels different. The air is thick with an impending weight, and my soul is heavy with what lies ahead.

The garden, with its tranquil beauty, feels almost surreal against the backdrop of my impending exit. In my mind I take a moment to breathe deeply, inhaling the scent of the earth and the foliage, allowing the serenity to wash over me. Yet, as I step further into its embrace, I can feel the storm within me intensifying. Each step toward the familiar clearing draws me closer to a reality I have known was coming, yet one I dread facing.

Once settled in a secluded spot, I fall to my knees, my heart racing with the weight of what is to come. I close my eyes and begin to pray, reaching out to the Father with all that I am. "Abba," I whisper, my voice trembling as I seek His presence. In this moment of vulnerability, I lay bare my fears and anxieties, pouring out my soul like water spilled upon the ground.

"Father, if you are willing, take this cup from me; yet not my will, but yours be done." The words echo in my mind, each syllable a reminder of the path laid before me. I am overwhelmed by the gravity of my mission, the suffering I know awaits me. My body trembles at the thought of the pain, the isolation, and the rejection I will face. Tears stream down my face as I grapple with the reality of my sacrifice.

The emotional struggle is unlike anything I have ever experienced. My heart aches not just for myself, but for those I love—my disciples who will be left to navigate their faith in my absence, and the world that so desperately needs hope and redemption. I feel the weight of their doubts and fears pressing upon me like an anchor, dragging me deeper into my anguish.

As I pray, I am reminded of the many moments we shared—the laughter, the teachings, the love. I think of Peter, James, and John, their loyalty and devotion, yet their inability to fully grasp the magnitude of this moment. I wish they could understand the depth of my struggle, the price that must be paid for the sake of love.

The intensity of my prayers rises; I cry out for strength, for clarity, for the courage to fulfill the will of the Father. I know that what lies ahead is not merely physical suffering but a deep spiritual battle—a confrontation with the weight of sin and separation from the divine. Each moment feels like an eternity as I wrestle with my purpose.

Suddenly, I feel a profound sense of isolation. Despite the beauty surrounding me, the garden feels eerily quiet, as if creation itself is holding its breath. I call out again, pleading for companionship, yearning for the support of my closest friends. But as I glance back toward the place where I left them, I see them slumped against the olive trees, heavy with sleep, unaware of the turmoil I face. My heart sinks; they cannot bear this burden with me, and the loneliness cuts deeper than any physical pain.

In that moment of profound isolation, I find a deeper resolve within me. I realize that this journey is mine alone, and though it feels unbearable, it is a path that must be walked. I stand once more, a wave of determination surging through me. I return to prayer, this time with a firmer voice. "Not my will, but yours be done." I reaffirm my commitment to the mission set before me, embracing the suffering that is to come as a necessary part of the greater story of love and redemption.

As I continue to pray, I feel a shift within—a subtle strength emerging from the depths of my despair. I remember the essence of my message: love, compassion, forgiveness. These are the very reasons I endure this pain. With each breath, I invite the Father's presence to fill the void, grounding me in the certainty of His love. I am reminded that even in the darkest moments, I am never truly alone.

The emotional tide begins to ebb, and as dawn approaches, I feel a newfound clarity. While my body remains tense with the anticipation of suffering, my spirit has found peace. I know that this is not just a moment of weakness but a testament to the profound connection between doubt and strength. It is through the struggle that I will emerge renewed, ready to fulfill the purpose for which I was sent.

In the stillness of the garden, I rise, feeling the warmth of the sun beginning to pierce the horizon. I take one last look around, embracing the beauty of this sacred place. The olive trees stand as witnesses to my journey, their roots intertwined with the earth, a symbol of resilience and strength.

With a final prayer of gratitude, I turn back to my disciples. It is time to face the storm that awaits. Though fear still lingers, I carry with me the lessons of Gethsemane—lessons of vulnerability, courage, and unwavering love. I step forward, ready to embrace the path ahead, trusting in the Father's will as I prepare to fulfill my mission.

The memory of the garden hurts as much as the burden I now carry. In Gethsemane, I felt the weight of my mission pressing down on me, grappling with fear and sorrow in the quiet of the night. The solace of those olive trees, once a refuge, now contrasts sharply with the cruelty I face. Each recollection of my anguished prayers and the disciples' troubled faces intensifies the pain of my current journey.

As I walk, I feel the echoes of my vulnerability and the love that surrounded me there, reminding me of the hope I cling to amidst this suffering. The garden represents both my deepest struggle and the profound connection I have to humanity. It is a bittersweet reminder that even in moments of despair, love can blossom, guiding me forward through the darkest valleys.

Memory has a way of looping back onto itself and again I find myself kneeling in the soft earth of Gethsemane, I notice my disciples just a short distance away. They are weary, their eyes heavy with sleep, the weight of the impending trial pressing down on them. I can't help but feel a surge of compassion for them. They are grappling with their own fears, trying to comprehend the storm that looms ahead. In this quiet, sacred space, their struggle mirrors my own, highlighting the shared human experience of uncertainty.

As I cast my gaze toward them, I see Peter, James, and John—the three who have been closest to me in these final days. They had witnessed my miracles, shared in my teachings, and felt the urgency of my mission. Yet now, their bodies betray them. Their heads droop, and their breaths come in slow, heavy sighs. I feel a pang of sorrow; they want to be there for me, but the weight of the night has overtaken their spirits.

"Could you not keep watch for one hour?" I ask, my voice barely above a whisper. It's a moment filled with love and understanding. They are not just my disciples; they are my friends, and I know their hearts. This is a pivotal moment for all of us, yet it is difficult for them to grasp the gravity of what is about to unfold.

In their sleep, I see reflections of my own struggles—doubt, fear, confusion. These feelings are universal, and their presence is a reminder that even the strongest among us can falter. Their struggle highlights our shared humanity, and in this realization, I find solace. We are all interconnected, bound by our vulnerabilities, and it is in these moments that true strength is often born.

Returning to my prayers, I feel the act of communicating with the Father transforming my doubt into resolve. With each breath, I pour out my heart, allowing the weight of my fears to dissipate into the night air. The solitude of Gethsemane wraps around me, and I sense the divine presence enveloping me, reassuring me that I am not alone in this struggle.

Through prayer, I begin to see my doubts in a new light. What once felt like an insurmountable burden now becomes a catalyst for strength. The honesty of my prayers allows me to confront my fears head-on, rather than letting them fester in the shadows. I realize that vulnerability is not a weakness; it is a powerful aspect of faith. In these moments of openness, I am not just asking for strength; I am inviting transformation.

As I stand to check on my disciples once more, I find that they are stirring, waking from their slumber. Their eyes meet mine, and I can see the concern etched on their faces. "We are here," they say, their voices soft but resolute. In their presence, I find encouragement, a reminder that even in our weakest moments, we are stronger together.

I share with them my experience of prayer—the way it has anchored me amidst uncertainty. I encourage them to lean into their fears, to find strength in their vulnerability. "Pray, so that you will not fall into temptation," I urge, knowing that they too will face trials in the days to come.

Together, we sit in the quiet of the garden, enveloped by the soft sounds of nature awakening. The dawn approaches, and with it, the promise of new beginnings. In this sacred moment, I impart the lesson I have learned: that even in moments of fear, prayer can transform our doubts into strength, guiding us through the darkness.

As the sun begins to rise, I feel a sense of renewal wash over me. I am filled with hope for my disciples, knowing that the struggles they face now will shape them into the leaders they are destined to become. In our shared vulnerability, we are united in purpose, ready to face the challenges ahead with unwavering faith and love. Together, we will carry this message of hope into the world, even as we approach the storm that awaits.

As I journey toward the culmination of my earthly mission, I find myself reflecting deeply on the nature of leadership. In these final moments, I grapple with the misconceptions that have long surrounded the role of a leader. So often, we equate leadership with an unwavering display of strength and authority, projecting an image of invincibility that others can admire and aspire to. But as I stand here, burdened yet hopeful, I recognize that true leadership is far more nuanced.

Vulnerability is not a weakness; it is a vital strength. It is the very thread that weaves together the fabric of connection, trust, and authenticity among those I have called to follow me. When I allowed myself to be open about my fears and doubts, I found a profound resonance in the hearts of my disciples. They saw that I, too, wrestled with the enormity of my mission, and in those shared moments of uncertainty, we forged a deeper bond.

I think back to times when I was overwhelmed by the expectations placed upon me—the pressure from religious leaders, the crowds clamoring for miracles, the weight of my own aspirations. Each moment was an opportunity for me to retreat into a façade of strength, but I chose instead to confront my vulnerabilities. I remember the honesty of my prayers in Gethsemane, when I bared my soul to the Father, and how that act of surrender became a turning point for me.

In opening myself up to my disciples about my struggles, I created a space for them to do the same. I think of Peter, who often wore his heart on his sleeve. By sharing my own fears, I encouraged him to acknowledge his. In our moments of shared vulnerability, we found strength. When Peter denied me, it was my understanding and compassion that ultimately led to his restoration. I recognized that true leadership is about lifting others up, guiding them through their darkest hours, and showing them that they are never alone.

Encouraging authenticity has been a cornerstone of my ministry. I have witnessed the transformative power of vulnerability among my followers. When they see a leader who is genuine about their struggles, they feel safe to embrace their own. This creates a resilient community where honesty reigns, and individuals are free to express their fears and doubts without judgment.

I remember the time I spoke to the crowd about the importance of love, compassion, and the challenges of discipleship. I shared my own trials, recounting how even I, the Son of Man, faced moments of doubt. The looks of understanding on their faces were profound. They knew that leadership is not about having all the answers but about navigating life's uncertainties together.

Vulnerability in leadership fosters resilience—not only in the leader but also in those they lead. When I acknowledged my own struggles, it invited my disciples to do the same. We became a united front against the challenges we faced. It is in these moments of honesty that we grow stronger together, forging bonds that will withstand the trials ahead.

As I reflect on my journey, I realize that the lessons I have learned about vulnerability will echo long after I am gone. My disciples will carry these insights into the world, embodying a leadership style rooted in authenticity and compassion. They will become leaders who are unafraid to show their true selves, to share their fears, and to connect with others on a deeper level.

In these final moments, I hope to leave them with this crucial understanding: that vulnerability is not a barrier to leadership but rather a bridge to deeper relationships. It is an invitation to engage in the struggles of life together, fostering a community built on trust, resilience, and love. As I take my last steps toward the cross, I carry this truth in my heart, knowing that my vulnerability has paved the way for a new kind of leadership—one that will inspire and transform in the years to come.

As I approach Golgotha, the culmination of my earthly journey, the paradox of strength found in weakness resonates deeply within me. In this moment of reflection, I recognize how my own struggles and doubts have shaped profound teachings that speak to the heart of the human experience. It is through my moments of vulnerability that I have discovered the true essence of strength, not as an absence of fear, but as a deep reliance on God during times of struggle.

I recall the times when the weight of my mission felt overwhelming—the crowds that pressed in, the relentless questioning of the religious leaders, the fear of abandonment by those I loved most. Each moment of doubt became an opportunity for growth, an invitation to turn inward and seek the strength that only God could provide. In those sacred moments, I learned that acknowledging my weaknesses did not diminish my purpose; rather, it illuminated the path forward.

This understanding of strength through weakness is a cornerstone of my teachings. I remember sharing with my disciples the importance of surrendering to God in times of trouble, emphasizing that our reliance on Him transforms our vulnerabilities into vessels of grace. In those moments when we feel the most powerless, we become open to the profound ways God can work through us. It is in our weakness that His power is made perfect.

I recall the agony in Gethsemane when the reality of the crucifixion loomed before me. As I knelt in prayer, the weight of fear and sorrow threatened to consume me. Yet, it was in that moment of vulnerability that I encountered God's presence most profoundly. By surrendering my will, I found a deep sense of peace and clarity—a strength that I could not have mustered on my own. I learned that true strength often arises when we allow ourselves to be vulnerable before God.

Through my teachings, I sought to convey to my disciples that they too would face moments of weakness and doubt. I encouraged them to embrace these experiences as opportunities for growth. I shared the truth that being honest about our struggles not only fosters connection but also cultivates a community of faith where we can uplift one another. In the face of challenges, we can remind each other that we are not alone, and together we can draw strength from God.

I often urged them to reflect on the stories of those who came before us—Moses, David, and Noah and Abraham—who faced their own struggles yet relied on God's strength to fulfill their callings. Their journeys remind us that our weaknesses do not disqualify us from being vessels of God's love and purpose; rather, they enhance our ability to empathize with others and share in their burdens.

As I contemplate the lessons learned in my own moments of doubt, I realize that the journey ahead for my disciples will be filled with trials that will test their faith. I pray that they remember the teachings of strength found in weakness, embracing their vulnerabilities as they carry the message of love into the world. They will encounter hardships, but if they remain rooted in God's grace, they will find the strength to persevere.

I want to leave behind the enduring truth that our moments of doubt and struggle can lead to profound revelations of strength. By embracing our vulnerabilities and relying on God, we open ourselves to His transformative power. In this paradox lies the essence of faith—finding strength in weakness, and in that, we become instruments of love and hope for a world in need. As I continue on this path to the cross, I carry with me the knowledge that even in my weakest moments, God's strength shines through, illuminating the way for all who seek Him.

A pain in my back as a soldier kicks me. I struggle to regain my footing as the pain mingles with the weight of the cross pressing down on my shoulders. Each breath feels labored, but within the agony, I sense a flicker of strength. The crowd jeers, but I focus on the faces I hold dear, those who believe in me and my message of love and forgiveness.

With each step, I again draw on the memories of those I've healed and the lives I've touched. Their hope fuels my resolve, reminding me that this journey is not in vain. I refuse to let the soldiers' brutality define my path; instead, I choose to embody the love I preach.

I glance back at the soldiers, their cruelty a reflection of a world lost in darkness, and I realize that my suffering can be a beacon of light for them too. I carry their burdens along with my own, praying that my sacrifice will awaken compassion in their hearts. As I press forward, I am determined to transform this pain into a testament of love that will resonate long after I am gone.

As I reflect on the path I have walked, the intertwining of doubt and strength emerges as a profound theme throughout my ministry. It is a journey marked by moments of deep vulnerability, where fear often whispered in my ear, yet faith became my steadfast companion.

Throughout my life, I have faced immense expectations—from the crowds, the religious leaders, and even from within my own heart. Each moment of uncertainty and fear has served not as a stumbling block, but as a stepping stone towards growth. I have come to understand that doubt is not an enemy of faith; rather, it can be an invitation to seek deeper truths and greater reliance on God. In moments of questioning, I found the space to grapple with my mission and connect more intimately with my Father.

As I prepare for the crucifixion, I recognize the beauty in vulnerability. The agony in Gethsemane taught me that surrendering my will does not signify weakness; instead, it reveals the strength of spirit to trust in God's plan. This lesson is one I wish to impart to all who walk this earth: true strength often emerges from moments of vulnerability. It is in the cracks of our human experience that light can enter, illuminating our path forward.

I invite you, dear ones, to embrace your own doubts and fears as integral parts of your faith journeys. It is easy to view uncertainty as a burden, but I encourage you to see it as a catalyst for transformation. When you acknowledge your struggles, you open the door to authentic connection with others and, more importantly, with God. Your vulnerabilities can lead to profound encounters with grace, allowing you to grow in ways you never thought possible.

As I share this final reflection, I extend an invitation to all who seek solace in their doubts. Allow your questions to guide you toward deeper understanding and reliance on the divine. Remember that in your moments of despair, you are not alone. God walks with you, just as He walked with me in darkest hours.

As a move forward, a powerful prayer comes to mind. Let us pray together:

Heavenly Father, I come before you with a humble heart, seeking strength and guidance for the journeys ahead. I pray for those who wrestle with doubt and fear, that they may find comfort in knowing that their struggles do not define them. Help them embrace their vulnerabilities and draw closer to You in their moments of uncertainty. May they find the courage to face their challenges, trusting in Your divine purpose for their lives. Amen.

Chapter 7: The Last Supper

As I enter the upper room, a sense of sacredness envelops me, mingling with the familiar warmth of companionship. The air is thick with anticipation and the rich aromas of the Passover feast, evoking memories of our shared journeys—the laughter, the miracles, the deep discussions under starlit skies. The room is modest, adorned with simple decorations, yet it feels like a sanctuary, a hallowed space where we will share our final moments together.

The flickering candlelight casts gentle shadows on the walls, creating an intimate atmosphere. The long table is set with unleavened bread and wine, symbols of our heritage and the covenant between God and His people. Each item on the table tells a story—a reminder of our roots in faith, of the struggles and triumphs that have brought us here. This gathering is not just about food; it is a celebration of our community, a family forged in love and purpose.

As I look around the table, my heart swells with love and sadness. I see the faces of my disciples—each one a reflection of the journey we've taken together. Peter, with his bold spirit; John, ever the beloved; James, steadfast and loyal. They have stood by me through trials and triumphs, and now, as I prepare to share the most profound teachings of my life, I feel the weight of what lies ahead. The reality of my impending sacrifice looms heavy, casting a shadow over this moment of joy.

Yet, amidst the sorrow, there is also a deep sense of peace. I am reminded of the purpose behind this gathering—to share not only a meal but also a legacy of love and service. This is the moment to impart the lessons that will guide them after I am gone. It is a time to reinforce the bonds that have been woven together through our shared experiences, to prepare them for the trials that will soon come.

As we settle into our places at the table, I feel a mixture of gratitude and grief. Gratitude for the love and friendship we have cultivated, and grief for the knowledge that our time together is coming to an end. The emotional weight of this moment is almost unbearable, yet it is essential. It is in these final moments that I hope to impart the essence of my message: that love, service, and sacrifice are at the heart of our faith.

I am overwhelmed by the profound sense of community that envelops us. This final meal is not merely a gathering of friends; it is the culmination of a journey marked by shared experiences, deep connections, and the unwavering support we have offered one another. Each disciple brings their own story, their own struggles, and their unique perspectives, yet together we form a tapestry of faith and love that has flourished over the years.

The bond forged with my disciples is unlike any other. We have walked dusty roads, shared meals, and faced challenges together. Each moment has added depth to our relationship—moments of laughter, times of doubt, and profound revelations. In this intimate setting, I feel the weight of our shared history, the love that has grown between us, and the sacrifices each has made along the way. This meal is an opportunity to celebrate that community, to acknowledge the journey we've undertaken together. It is a moment to reflect on how our individual paths have converged into one mission. I cherish the distinct personalities at the table: Peter's impetuosity, John's gentle spirit, and James' steadfastness. Together, they embody the richness of our fellowship, a bond that will carry them forward even in my absence.

In this moment, I want them to understand the power of unity. The world outside these walls is fraught with division and conflict, but here, in this sacred space, we are reminded of the strength that comes from standing together. This is a final opportunity to reinforce the importance of love and support as they prepare to carry on the mission that we have begun.

As we gather for this meal, the significance of the Passover resonates deeply within me. This feast is a pivotal moment in Jewish tradition, a remembrance of liberation from bondage in Egypt and a celebration of God's faithfulness. It is a time when families come together to recount the story of their deliverance, to remember the lamb whose blood marked their doors, protecting them from death.

In this context, our gathering takes on an added layer of meaning. I am not only sharing a meal with my disciples; I am invoking a tradition that speaks to salvation, freedom, and divine providence. As we partake of the bread and wine,

I see them as symbols of something greater—an invitation to enter into a new covenant, one that will redefine their understanding of sacrifice and love.

The elements of this feast—the bread and wine—will soon transform in meaning, serving as a poignant reminder of my impending sacrifice. The connection to the Passover reminds us that our God is a God of redemption, and just as the Israelites were delivered from slavery, so too will humanity be offered salvation through my sacrifice.

As I look around the table, the emotions swirl within me—joy, sorrow, anticipation, and dread. This gathering is steeped in significance, yet it is tinged with the knowledge that it will be our last. The love I feel for my disciples is palpable, and I am struck by the bittersweet nature of this moment. I want to impart wisdom, to guide them through the uncertainties that lie ahead, yet the weight of my own impending sacrifice looms large.

In this final meal, I seek to cultivate an atmosphere of warmth and connection, to reassure my disciples that their mission will continue, even in the face of adversity. I want them to feel the depth of my love and the certainty of my teachings. As I prepare to share these final moments, I remind myself that this gathering is not an end, but rather a new beginning—a launching point for a movement rooted in love and service.

I invite my disciples to engage deeply with this moment, to cherish the fellowship we have built and to understand the sacredness of what we are about to share. This is not just a meal; it is a sacred celebration of community, faith, and the promise of redemption that lies ahead. Here, in this upper room, we are bound together by a shared purpose and a commitment to carry forward the message of love that transcends even the darkest of circumstances.

I am acutely aware that this will be the last time we share a meal together in this way. The gravity of this knowledge hangs heavily in the air, mingling with the aromas of the feast before us. Each bite taken feels imbued with an urgency that underscores the importance of our time together. I look into the faces of those I have come to love deeply, and I realize that each moment we have shared has led us to this pivotal gathering.

The thought of saying goodbye is almost unbearable. I reflect on the journey we have taken—the laughter, the challenges, and the sacred moments that have woven our lives together. Each disciple brings their own story, their struggles, and their victories, and I know that soon, they will face a world that will challenge their faith in ways they cannot yet imagine. This meal is not just a farewell; it is a preparation for what is to come, a moment to impart wisdom that will sustain them through the trials ahead.

In this atmosphere of impending separation, I feel a profound sense of urgency. There is so much I want to share, so much I want them to understand. I yearn to instill in them the importance of love and service, to remind them that our mission does not end with my departure. As the weight of my impending sacrifice looms, I want to equip them with the tools they will need to carry on without me.

The air is thick with emotion—anticipation mixed with sorrow. I sense the urgency in my heart, a drive to ensure that my disciples grasp the significance of the teachings I am about to impart. I want them to feel the depth of my love, to understand that even as I prepare to face the unimaginable, my commitment to them remains unwavering.

As I look around the table, I see the expressions of confusion and concern on their faces. They cannot yet comprehend the full weight of what is about to transpire. I feel a pang of sadness knowing that soon, they will grapple with feelings of fear and abandonment. My love for them compels me to address their unspoken worries, to reassure them that they will never be alone.

This moment is a sacred intersection of love and urgency, where the significance of our shared journey converges with the reality of my impending sacrifice. I know that the next steps I take will change everything, but I am determined to fill this room with hope, a hope that transcends the pain we are about to face.

In the midst of this farewell, I seek to create an atmosphere of belonging and support. I want my disciples to feel the strength of our bond, to understand that they are not just followers but beloved friends and companions. This meal is a reminder of our shared mission, a celebration of the love that will carry them forward.

I pray that they will hold on to the lessons of love and service that I have taught them. The urgency in my heart drives me to share these teachings, to reinforce the idea that love is the foundation of everything we have built together. I hope they will remember that our shared experiences, our laughter, our tears, and our sacrifices are what will sustain them as they continue this journey without me.

In this upper room, surrounded by those I hold dear, I prepare to share not just food, but a legacy—a legacy rooted in love, sacrifice, and unwavering faith.

Here, at this pivotal moment, we are bound together by our shared purpose, and it is my hope that they will carry this bond into the world beyond these walls, embodying the love we have cultivated together.

A profound sense of purpose fills my heart. It is in this sacred space that I choose to demonstrate the essence of love and service through an act that defies the conventions of the world. The moment is ripe for teaching, and I know I must embody the principles I have imparted throughout my ministry.

I rise from the table, feeling the weight of the moment pressing upon me. I take a basin of water and a towel, my heart heavy yet resolute. As I kneel before my disciples, I am aware that this act will not only serve as a lesson but also a powerful reminder of the love that must guide their future.

I begin with Peter, who looks at me with confusion and resistance. "Lord, are you going to wash my feet?" he asks, struggling to reconcile my actions with his understanding of my role as the Messiah. I meet his gaze, knowing that this is a moment of transformation. "Unless I wash you, you have no part with me," I reply, emphasizing the necessity of humility in our relationship.

As I wash each disciple's feet, I feel an overwhelming connection to them. Each foot I cleanse symbolizes not just their physical journeys but also the spiritual paths they are about to embark on. I take my time, pouring out love and care, recognizing that this moment signifies the depth of my commitment to them. This is not merely an act of service; it is a profound expression of the love I hold for each of them.

When I finish, I return to my place at the table, and I look around at their astonished faces. "Do you understand what I have done for you?" I ask, my voice steady yet filled with emotion. I explain that I, their teacher and Lord, have set an example for them—a model of humility and servant leadership. "Now that I, your Lord and Teacher, have washed your feet, you also should wash one another's feet," I declare, urging them to carry this lesson into their lives.

In this simple act of washing feet, I reveal a truth that transcends time: true leadership is rooted in service. I think of the world they will face—a world filled with power struggles, ambition, and the temptation to elevate oneself above others. I want them to remember this moment, to internalize the importance of serving one another with love and grace.

The act of washing feet also speaks to the heart my life—the message of love that knows no bounds. It is a radical call to humility, a reminder that in the Kingdom of God, greatness is found in selfless service. I reflect on the countless moments we have shared, the lessons I have taught, and the love that has grown among us. This moment encapsulates everything I have strived to impart.

As I look into their eyes, I see a flicker of understanding beginning to emerge. They may not grasp the full weight of this moment just yet, but I pray it will linger in their hearts. I want them to understand that love is not merely a feeling; it is an action—an intentional choice to place the needs of others above one's own.

I also consider the broader implications of this teaching. This act of service will echo through the ages, inspiring generations to embrace humility and love as central tenets of their faith. In a world often defined by selfishness, I hope my disciples will carry this message of servant leadership into the hearts of those they encounter, transforming lives through love.

As we return to our meal, I sense the atmosphere shifting. The gravity of what I have just demonstrated weighs heavily on us all. Love and service are not abstract concepts; they are the foundation of our community and the essence of our mission. I am determined to ensure that this lesson resonates with my disciples, guiding them in their journey ahead.

In this final gathering, I pray that they will embrace this calling to serve one another. My heart swells with hope as I envision a future where they embody the love we have shared, a love that transcends boundaries and transforms lives. The washing of their feet will forever remain a poignant reminder of the power of humility and the beauty of serving one another in love.

As we settle back into our meal, the atmosphere thick with emotion and anticipation, I know it is time to impart one of my most profound teachings—the commandment of love. I look around at my beloved disciples, each one a vital thread in the tapestry of my ministry, and I feel a surge of love for them that transcends words.

"Children, I am with you only a little longer," I begin, feeling the weight of what is to come. I want them to remember this moment, to hold it close as they navigate the trials that lie ahead. "A new command I give you: Love one another. As I have loved you, so you must love one another."

These words hang in the air, each syllable imbued with the essence of my message. I pause to let the gravity of the commandment sink in. "By this, everyone will know that you are my disciples, if you love one another." I see the mixture of understanding and uncertainty in their eyes, and I know I must elaborate on the depth of this love.

I reflect on the nature of the love I have shared with them—a love that is sacrificial, unconditional, and transformative. This is not a fleeting emotion; it is a deep commitment to the well-being of one another. It is a love that chooses to see beyond differences, beyond failures, and beyond fears. It is a love that bears all things, believes all things, hopes all things, and endures all things.

As I speak, I think about the moments we have shared—the laughter, the lessons, the struggles. Each experience has woven us together in a bond that is unbreakable. This love must be the cornerstone of their community. It will guide them through the trials of betrayal, fear, and uncertainty that they will inevitably face.

"Understand this," I urge them, "to love as I have loved you means to place others' needs above your own, to serve without expectation, and to forgive without reservation." I share the depth of my commitment to them, knowing that my sacrifice is the ultimate expression of this love. It is a love that will compel them to act, to reach out to the marginalized, and to embrace the outcasts.

I want them to grasp the immense responsibility that comes with this commandment. The world they will step into is rife with division and hostility, and it will be their love that stands as a testament to my presence among them. I emphasize that their love for one another will be their greatest witness, a reflection of the very heart of God.

"This commandment will not always be easy to follow," I acknowledge, my voice steady yet filled with compassion. "You will face challenges that test your resolve, moments that will ignite fear and doubt. But remember, love is a choice—a daily commitment to see each other through the lens of grace."

I see the questions flickering in their eyes—how can they embody such love? What if they falter? I reassure them that it is okay to struggle; it is through those struggles that their love will grow deeper and stronger. They will learn to lean on one another, to seek support in their moments of weakness, and to embody the very love I have shown them.

I feel a profound sense of hope wash over me. I know that this commandment will resonate throughout their lives, shaping their actions and decisions long after I am gone. They will carry this message into the world, and in doing so, they will fulfill their calling as my disciples.

This commandment is not merely an instruction; it is a lifeline, a guiding principle that will sustain them through the storms to come. It is an invitation to live boldly and authentically, to love fiercely, and to build a community that reflects the heart of God. My heart swells with pride and love for them as I entrust them with this sacred charge.

As the meal progresses, I feel the weight of what is about to unfold. I gather my thoughts, knowing that this moment will be etched in their hearts forever. I take a deep breath, feeling the presence of the Holy Spirit surrounding us, and prepare to share the most sacred of symbols—bread and wine.

I lift the loaf of bread, its surface warm and inviting. "This is my body, given for you," I say, breaking the bread with deliberate care. The sound of the crack echoes softly in the room, a reminder of the sacrifice I am about to make. "Every time you eat this bread, remember me." I look into their eyes, searching for understanding, knowing the depth of this moment will only be fully grasped in time.

The bread represents nourishment, the sustenance that will carry them through the trials ahead. It symbolizes my presence in their lives, the way I have walked beside them, taught them, and loved them unconditionally. "In partaking of this bread, you acknowledge our bond, the unity we share as one body in Christ."

Next, I take the cup, filled with rich, deep wine. "This cup is the new covenant in my blood, which is poured out for you." I watch their faces as the significance of my words begins to dawn on them. The cup represents the promise of forgiveness, redemption, and the new relationship with God that my sacrifice will establish.

I extend the cup towards them, my heart heavy with emotion. "Drink from it, all of you; this is my blood of the covenant, which is poured out for many for the forgiveness of sins." In this moment, I invite them into something profound—a shared experience that transcends time and space.

I explain the importance of this new covenant, a radical shift from the old ways of sacrifice and ritual. This covenant embodies grace and mercy, a promise that no longer relies on the law but on my love and sacrifice. I want them to understand that this is not just a ritual; it is an invitation to enter into a deeper relationship with me and with each other.

"Each time you gather and break bread, remember this moment," I urge them. "Let it be a reminder of my love and the mission I am entrusting to you." I want them to carry this sacred act forward, to use it as a touchstone for their faith and a source of strength in the times to come.

As they take the bread and sip from the cup, I am filled with a mix of sorrow and hope. I know the road ahead will be fraught with challenges, yet in this sacred act, they are also receiving a promise—a promise of presence, strength, and unity.

This moment signifies more than just the sharing of a meal; it is a profound declaration of faith and commitment. It is a reminder that they are part of a larger story, one that encompasses love, sacrifice, and redemption. In their act of communion, they acknowledge their role as my disciples, called to carry forth the message of love into a world in desperate need of hope.

As the bread and wine pass among them, I pray they feel the gravity of what we are sharing. This is a moment that transcends the ordinary, a divine encounter that will sustain them through the darkest valleys. It is a reminder that they are never alone—that my body and blood will be their strength, their guide, and their source of comfort.

I close my eyes briefly, taking in the weight of this moment, knowing that the implications of this gathering will echo through the ages. As they consume the bread and wine, I trust that they will carry the essence of our shared love and sacrifice into the world, becoming vessels of my grace and peace.

As I am tripped by a soldier, I fall hard onto the dusty road, the impact jolting through my body. The coarse earth scratches my skin, and for a moment, I feel the world spin around me. Pain radiates from my bruised limbs, but it's the weight of the cross that pins me down, making it nearly impossible to rise.

I struggle against the crushing burden, my muscles screaming in protest, yet I refuse to stay on the ground. With every ounce of strength, I push myself up, but the heavy wood feels like an anchor, holding me in place.

In this vulnerable moment, I feel the eyes of the crowd upon me—some filled with scorn, others with pity. I close my eyes briefly, recalling the love I carry within, drawing on the memories of those who have shown me kindness. This suffering is

profound, but it is not the end. I gather my resolve, determined to stand, knowing that each moment of struggle is a step closer to fulfilling my purpose. I can't stand.
As the meal continues, a heaviness settles in the room, a palpable shift in the atmosphere. I know that what I am about to reveal will change everything. The joy and camaraderie we've shared during this final meal will be overshadowed by a dark truth that looms over us like a storm cloud.

"I must tell you the truth," I begin, my voice steady but filled with sorrow. "One of you will betray me." The words hang in the air, thick and suffocating, as I watch the reactions unfold before me. I can see the confusion on their faces, the disbelief as they process the enormity of my statement.

The shock ripples through the group like a wave, each disciple grappling with the implications of my words. Peter's face hardens in determination; he shakes his head, unwilling to accept what I have just said. John, ever the sensitive soul, glances around the table, searching for answers in the eyes of his fellow disciples. A tension rises, a mixture of fear and disbelief, as each one wonders how such a betrayal could happen among us.

"Surely not I, Lord?" echoes from several lips, a chorus of denial. I can feel their pain, their distress, and it mirrors my own. This moment is a crucible, revealing not just the fragility of trust but the deep bonds we have formed over our time together.

The reactions are as varied as the men before me. Some sit in stunned silence, grappling with the reality of betrayal from within our circle. Others murmur among themselves, doubt creeping into their hearts. I sense Peter's protective instinct rising, his desire to defend our fellowship and confront the one who would dare to turn against me.

"Is it I, Lord?" Judas asks, his voice a mixture of defiance and vulnerability. I meet his gaze, and in that moment, I see the conflict within him—the struggle between the darkness that beckons and the light he has witnessed. "You have said so," I reply, my heart heavy. I want him to know that even in this moment, I do not turn away from him.

The tension in the room grows as I contemplate the gravity of Judas's decision. I remember the moments we shared, the laughter, the teachings, and the bond we formed. It pains me to know that he has allowed greed and fear to overshadow the love we once nurtured.

In their confusion, the disciples begin to draw closer to me, seeking reassurance. I see their loyalty, their love, and it breaks my heart to know what is to come. I wish I could shield them from this pain, from the reality that one among them will turn away.

This moment feels like a dark shadow cast over our gathering, a reminder of the fragility of human relationships. I am reminded that even among those closest to us, the seeds of betrayal can take root. Yet, I must hold firm to the truth that love can endure even the most profound betrayals.

I look around the table, my heart aching for each of them. "The Son of Man goes as it has been written about him," I say softly, my voice tinged with sadness. "But woe to that man who betrays the Son of Man! It would be better for him if he had not been born." The weight of these words sinks into the silence, a sobering reminder of the path we are on.

In this moment, I feel the urgency to impart wisdom to my disciples. I want them to understand that betrayal does not negate the love we have shared. It does not erase the purpose of our journey together. "You must love one another, even when it is hard," I urge, hoping to instill a sense of resilience within them. "In the face of betrayal, let love be your guide."

As I reflect on their reactions—shock, confusion, fear—I am reminded of the humanity we all share. We are not immune to the darkness that can creep into our hearts. This moment will test their faith, their resolve, and their understanding of what it means to love and serve. It will challenge them to rise above the pain of betrayal and find strength in unity.

I know this moment will leave a lasting imprint on their hearts. They will remember this final gathering, this shared meal, and the weight of betrayal that hung in the air. I pray that, despite the pain, they will carry forward the lessons of love and resilience, finding hope even in the darkest of times.

I can't stand, crushed by the burdened. Crushed by the weight of the cross and the physical toll of my suffering, I sense the crowd pressing in around me. Among the jeering soldiers and onlookers, I catch a glimpse of someone emerging from the throng.

He approaches hesitantly, drawn by the sight of my struggle and the compassion in his heart. The soldiers, perhaps feeling the urgency of the moment, suddenly command him to help me stand and carry the heavy cross. At first, Simon of Cyrene appears reluctant, likely taken aback by the violence and chaos surrounding us, but the desperation in my eyes compels him forward.

As he steps closer, I see his determination grow. He takes hold of the cross, sharing its weight as I lean into his support. In that instant, our connection deepens—two lives intersecting in a moment of profound empathy. Simon's assistance not only alleviates my burden but also transforms his path. He becomes an unexpected participant in my journey, a symbol of the compassion that can arise even amid suffering.

Together, we move forward, Simon's presence a reminder that even in our darkest hours, there are those willing to lend a hand, to share in the pain, and to walk alongside us.

As Simon bears the weight of the cross, I can feel the strain in his muscles, the burden pressing down on him. I glance at him, my heart heavy with gratitude and pain.

"Thank you," I whisper, my voice barely a breath. "You carry a heavy load for me."

He nods, sweat glistening on his brow, determination etched on his face. "I won't let you fall. I can feel your suffering. It's... it's overwhelming."

"Stay strong," I urge, feeling the weight of both the cross and the world pressing against us. "This is not just my burden; it's for all who suffer. You're part of something greater."

Simon's brow furrows, and he looks up at me, eyes searching. "What do you mean? This pain... it feels endless."

"It is," I reply, struggling to keep my focus. "But through this suffering, love will emerge. Redemption awaits on the other side."

He glances around at the crowd, confusion mingling with compassion. "I'm just a man, not a savior. How can I help?"

"Your strength in this moment is a testament to the power of love," I say, my voice trembling. "Every act of kindness matters, Simon. You carry hope for others, even when you feel lost."

He takes a deep breath, adjusting his grip on the cross. "I can feel it now... the weight of it all. But your words give me strength."

"Then carry that strength with you," I encourage, my heart swelling with gratitude. "Know that you are not alone. We walk this path together, and in our suffering, we are united."

As we continue, I can see the resolve in Simon's eyes. Though the journey is long and fraught with pain, I hold onto the belief that love and sacrifice will light the way for all who follow.

I glance at the strength of Simon and my mind turns back to Judas. A complex tapestry of emotions unfurls within me. Simon is a stranger. Judas was one of my chosen, a member of our close-knit community. Yet, beneath the surface of our fellowship lies a profound struggle—a conflict that ultimately leads him down a path of betrayal.

Judas Iscariot, the keeper of the money bag, was not just a disciple; he was a man filled with ambition and longing. I think back to the moments when he first joined us, the eager look in his eyes as he heard my teachings and witnessed the miracles. There was a time when I believed he would be a pillar of strength among us. But over time, I sensed a shift—a growing discontent that clouded his heart.

What were his motivations? Was it greed that drove him to betray me? The thirty pieces of silver, a paltry sum in exchange for the bond we shared. Or was it something deeper, a longing for power, recognition, or perhaps a misguided belief that he could force my hand to fulfill the role of a revolutionary leader? I wonder if he felt trapped, caught between the weight of expectation and the allure of his own ambitions.

In the quiet of this moment, I am struck by the tragic nature of Judas' journey. He is a mirror reflecting the struggles we all face—the battle between light and darkness, love and betrayal. I want to reach out to him, to pull him back from the brink, but I know that the choice lies with him. Each of us has a choice to make, a path to follow, and sadly, he has chosen a path that will lead to his own undoing.

Then, the moment of heartbreak arrives. I see Judas stand up, a familiar face now tinged with a darkness that feels almost foreign. The room, once filled with the warmth of camaraderie, grows colder as he approaches me, the weight of his decision palpable in the air.

"I will give him a kiss," he had said to the chief priests and officers, and I know that this moment is upon us. The act, simple yet loaded with betrayal, is an intimate gesture twisted into an instrument of deception.

As he steps forward, time seems to slow. The other disciples are oblivious to the gravity of what is unfolding. They trust him, still believing in the bond we share.

But I see through the façade, and my heart aches for what is to come. "Judas," I say softly, my voice barely above a whisper. "Are you betraying the Son of Man with a kiss?" The weight of the question hangs in the air, filled with sorrow and disbelief.

In that instant, the atmosphere shifts dramatically. The warmth of our gathering dissipates, replaced by an overwhelming tension. I can see the shock wash over the faces of my disciples as they grasp the reality of the situation. Confusion gives way to fear, and fear morphs into a desperate desire to protect what we have built together.

As Judas leans in, the kiss becomes a symbol of betrayal, an act that will reverberate through time. The eyes of the other disciples widen in disbelief, and I can almost hear the collective gasp as they begin to comprehend the depth of his actions. Peter's hand instinctively moves toward his sword, a protective reflex born from love and confusion.

In this moment, the room is filled with a cacophony of emotions—shock, grief, anger, and betrayal. I feel the weight of each disciple's pain as they confront the reality that one of their own has chosen a path of treachery. This moment is not just a betrayal of me, but of the very trust that binds us together.

As I watch Judas step back, a sense of finality settles in. I know that our paths are diverging irreversibly. I pray for him, even in this moment of heartbreak, hoping that he will find a way back to the love he has turned away from. But deep down, I sense that he is already lost, ensnared by the darkness he has allowed to take root in his heart.

This moment of betrayal casts a long shadow over the Last Supper, forever altering the trajectory of our shared journey. It serves as a reminder of the fragility of trust and the depths of human choice. In the aftermath, I am left with a profound sense of sorrow—not just for myself, but for Judas, for the choices he has made, and for the love that he has forsaken.

I gather my thoughts amidst the chaos, I resolve to turn this moment into a lesson for the others—a lesson about the power of love, the danger of ambition, and the importance of staying true to the path of light, even when darkness seeks to consume us.

As the weight of Judas' betrayal sinks in, I find myself grappling with an emotional turmoil that is as profound as it is painful. This is not merely the act of a friend turning against me; it is a rupture in the very fabric of our shared journey—a heart-wrenching reminder of how love can sometimes give way to treachery.

In that moment, I feel an ache that cuts deeper than any physical wound. Judas was not just a disciple; he was someone I had poured my heart into, sharing with him not only teachings but also my life. We laughed together, prayed together, and journeyed together through trials and triumphs. To have that bond severed by his choice feels like a dagger to my heart.

The tears I hold back are not just for myself, but for him as well. I know that his betrayal stems from a place of conflict, one that I have witnessed in others but never expected to see in Judas. The trust I extended to him now feels like a fragile glass, shattered by a single moment of greed and ambition. It is a painful reminder that the path of faith is fraught with human frailty, and even the closest relationships can be tested in the most unexpected ways.

This moment encapsulates the profound struggle between love and betrayal—a tension that has echoed throughout my ministry. Love, I have taught, is meant to be unconditional, a reflection of the divine connection we share. Yet here I stand, confronted with the stark reality that even love can be weaponized, twisted into an instrument of betrayal.

As I look around at my disciples, I see their faces pale with shock, confusion written across their features. Each one is grappling with their own emotions, their understanding of loyalty and trust being challenged. The atmosphere in the room shifts, turning heavy and charged, as if the very air we breathe has become laden with the weight of our collective sorrow.

I reflect on the lesson this moment holds for all of us. It is a stark reminder that betrayal can come from those we hold dear, and that trust is not a guarantee. Yet, even in the midst of this pain, I must hold fast to the truth that love remains the greatest commandment. It is my hope that this experience will deepen their understanding of what it means to love—what it truly means to lay down one's life for a friend.

In this moment, I understand that love is not just a feeling; it is a choice, a commitment that often demands sacrifice. The juxtaposition of love and betrayal illuminates the very heart of the human experience—a struggle that we all face in our relationships.

As I ponder these truths, I feel the familiar presence of the Father surrounding me, a comforting reminder that love can still prevail, even in the darkest of circumstances. I recognize that while Judas may have chosen to turn away, I am called to continue loving, to embody the very essence of grace even when it is most difficult.

The emotional impact of this moment transcends my personal pain; it resonates deeply with the theme of trust versus treachery that has woven itself through our journey. I realize that every interaction, every teaching moment, has led us to this juncture. Trust is a delicate dance, requiring vulnerability and a willingness to be seen, and yet it is fragile, easily shattered by the weight of betrayal.

I find myself reflecting on the nature of leadership and the expectations that accompany it. To lead is to open oneself to the possibility of hurt, to extend love and trust even when the outcome is uncertain. It is a daunting task, but one that I have embraced, knowing that the greatest commandment is to love fiercely and without reservation.

As I look into the faces of my disciples, I resolve to use this moment not only as a lesson in betrayal but as an opportunity to reinforce the importance of community, love, and resilience. Together, we must confront the reality of our humanity—the imperfections, the doubts, and yes, even the betrayals that can arise from within our midst.

This evening, as we share our final meal, I choose to focus on love's enduring power. I hope that this experience will strengthen their bonds and inspire them to carry the message of love into a world that desperately needs it. In the face of betrayal, we must remember that love can heal, transform, and ultimately prevail.

And yet, I hold close the hope that even in this painful moment, a greater purpose will emerge—one that speaks to the depth of love and the transformative power of forgiveness. In this garden of trust, where shadows of betrayal loom large, I reaffirm my commitment to love unconditionally, knowing that it is love that will ultimately define our legacy.

As I contemplate the significance of this gathering, I am acutely aware of the lasting legacy it will leave. This meal is more than a farewell; it is the establishment of a new ritual—one that will serve as a reminder of the love and sacrifice I have offered. I envision future disciples breaking bread and sharing wine in remembrance of me, in a communal act that transcends time and space.

In this moment, I am filled with hope that my teachings will take root in their hearts, guiding them as they navigate the challenges ahead. The commandment to "love one another as I have loved you" will become a guiding principle for their lives and for the communities they will build. This legacy of love will be the thread that weaves through the fabric of the Church, binding believers together in a shared commitment to serve and uplift one another.

I feel a sense of peace as I acknowledge that while my earthly ministry is drawing to a close, the impact of our time together will endure. The bonds formed in this room, the lessons imparted, and the love shared will resonate in the hearts of those who choose to follow in my footsteps. I trust that my disciples will carry forth this legacy, even in the face of adversity and betrayal.

In these final moments, I look into the eyes of each disciple, conveying a message of unwavering love and commitment. I know that the path ahead will be fraught with challenges, but I trust that they will embody the teachings of love and service that I have imparted. Together, we are not merely sharing a meal; we are forging a covenant that will change the course of history.

As the Last Supper comes to a close, I feel a sense of gratitude for this sacred time we have shared. In this space of communion, I invite my disciples to remember the importance of love, sacrifice, and community. Though my physical presence may soon fade, the spirit of this meal will endure, inspiring generations to come to live out the values we have cherished together.

Chapter 8: The Trial

As I stand at the precipice of this moment, the atmosphere is charged with tension, a palpable weight hanging in the air. The trial unfolds under the harsh glow of torches that flicker like uncertain hopes amidst a sea of confusion and anger. Religious leaders—clad in their ornate robes, faces set in stern determination—huddle together, their whispers weaving a web of accusations and deceit. They have come prepared, intent on solidifying their power, ready to snuff out the light that has illuminated so many hearts.

The crowd swells around the trial, a turbulent mass of faces reflecting a spectrum of emotions: fear, curiosity, and an unsettling eagerness for spectacle. Some among them are my followers, faces etched with disbelief and sorrow, while others are fueled by the fiery rhetoric of the chief priests, their minds twisted by misunderstanding and fear. The air is thick with the scent of dust and sweat, a reminder of the human struggle that binds us all together in this chaotic moment.

Soldiers stand guard, their armor clinking softly with each movement, creating a jarring contrast to the solemnity of the proceedings. Their eyes scan the crowd, ever vigilant, while their presence amplifies the atmosphere of intimidation. This is not merely a trial; it is a demonstration of power, an assertion of control by those who fear the change I have represented.

As I face my accusers, I am acutely aware of the gravity of this moment. My heart feels heavy, not only with the weight of their accusations but with the realization that this gathering marks a turning point in human history. This is the culmination of a journey filled with miracles, teachings, and love, now reduced to a series of baseless charges meant to erase the very essence of my mission.

I am struck by the irony of this moment—the very people who should seek truth and justice are instead wrapped in a shroud of fear and envy. They have turned away from the light I have brought, choosing instead the shadows of deceit and betrayal. It is here, amidst the clamor and chaos, that I find myself grappling with the profound implications of humanity's choice to misunderstand and malign.

I meditate deep into the heart of this trial—an exploration of the injustices faced, the fear that drives humanity to such extremes, and the silent strength I draw from my faith. This moment is not just a personal trial but a reflection of the broader human condition, a testament to the struggle between light and darkness.

As I stand in the courtroom and gaze out at the crowd, a wave of emotions washes over me. I see familiar faces twisted with anger, others filled with confusion and doubt. My heart aches as I recognize those who have followed me, now caught in a whirlwind of fear and manipulation.

The accusations directed at me feel heavy and unjust, and I wonder how so much misunderstanding has taken root in their hearts. I am struck by the irony of it all—those I came to save are now my accusers, lost in their own turmoil.

Amidst the noise, I feel a profound sadness for their blindness, for the love I have shared seems overshadowed by fear and hatred. Yet, I remind myself that this moment is not just about my suffering; it is about the hope of redemption for all.

In this courtroom, I resolve to remain steadfast, to embody the very message of love and forgiveness that brought me here. I must show them, through my silence and grace, that even in the face of injustice, love can triumph over darkness.

A swirl of initial thoughts and emotions washes over me. There is a profound weight in my chest, an ache that resonates with the reality of what is unfolding. I feel the intensity of their gazes, sharp as daggers, filled with hostility and suspicion. In this charged atmosphere, I recognize the gravity of the moment—not only for myself but for the very essence of what I have sought to teach and embody.

The air is thick with anticipation, and as I lock eyes with the chief priests and elders, I am struck by the contrast between their fervor and the quiet resolve within me. I sense their desperation to maintain control, to silence a voice that has challenged their authority and revealed the truth of their hearts. The accusations against me—blasphemy, heresy—ring hollow, echoing with the dissonance of misunderstanding. Yet I stand firm, not in defiance, but in a deep commitment to my mission.

This trial is more than a personal reckoning; it is a microcosm of humanity's struggle with fear and ignorance. It encapsulates the tendency to distort truth when faced with discomfort, to lash out against what we cannot comprehend. I feel a deep sorrow for those who seek to condemn me, for they are blinded by their own fears and insecurities.

The purpose of these reflections is to provide insight into the nature of this trial—its profound injustices, the human emotions at play, and the broader implications for humanity. I wish to illuminate the lessons embedded within this moment, showcasing how fear can warp understanding and lead to actions that ripple through time. As I prepare to face my accusers, I invite you to journey with me through this experience, to witness the layers of betrayal, the clashing of faith and fear, and the unwavering strength that emerges in the face of adversity.

In this crucible, I will reflect on the very heart of what it means to stand firm in faith, even when the world around me threatens to pull me under. The essence of this trial will reveal not only my steadfastness but also the profound implications for all of humanity, a call to recognize the shadows within ourselves and to seek the light that leads to redemption.

As I stand before the high priest and the gathered crowd, my heart is heavy with a storm of emotions. Confusion and sorrow intertwine as I hear the false accusations hurled against me. It pains me deeply to witness those I've loved turning against me, their faces twisted by fear and misunderstanding.

Simultaneously, the agony of carrying the cross weighs down not just on my shoulders but on my spirit. Each step sends sharp pain through my body, reminding me of the physical suffering I endure. Yet, in this crucible of trial, I feel a profound resolve rising within me. I know that this moment is part of a greater purpose, and I must remain steadfast in my mission.

As I face my accusers, I am filled with compassion for their blindness, recognizing their struggle with doubt and fear. I hold onto the love that has driven me throughout my life, drawing strength from the memories of those I have healed and comforted. In this moment of anguish, I am determined to embody that love, showing that even in the depths of despair, hope and redemption can prevail.

The accusations are read aloud: blasphemy for claiming divine status, disrupting the peace of Jerusalem, and inciting rebellion against Roman rule.

Each charge feels like a blow, striking not just at my character but at the very essence of my mission.

The proclamation that I am "King of the Jews" resonates with the crowd. It is a title that carries weight, both politically and spiritually. They misunderstand my kingship, conflating it with earthly power rather than the profound truth of love and service I have come to embody.

As I listen to the accusations, I cannot help but reflect on the motivations behind them. The religious leaders, fearful of losing their influence, see me as a challenger to their status quo. Their jealousy blinds them to the truth I have been revealing—a truth that calls for transformation rather than mere adherence to tradition.

Their actions stem from a place of fear. They fear the loss of their power, the disruption of their carefully constructed systems, and the awakening of the people to a new understanding of faith. This fear breeds hostility, leading them to conspire against me rather than seek understanding or reconciliation.

I also see the broader human tendency at play—how fear can drive individuals to cling to the familiar, to resist change, and to scapegoat those who challenge their beliefs. It is a painful reflection of humanity's struggle to embrace truth when it disrupts comfort.

In this moment of accusation, I feel a deep sadness for those who stand against me. Their fear has closed their hearts to love and possibility, leading them down a path of condemnation rather than compassion. Yet, I remain resolute in my purpose, understanding that my mission transcends these accusations. I will respond not with anger but with grace, embodying the very teachings I have shared with my disciples.

As the trial unfolds, I recognize the deeper implications of this moment—not just for me, but for all who will come to know my story. It serves as a reminder of the necessity of love in the face of fear, and the call to rise above misunderstanding with courage and compassion.

But I feel a deep pain in my heart, a profound ache that comes from not being seen for who I truly am. The crowd's faces, once filled with admiration, are now clouded by fear and misunderstanding. They reduce me to a mere blasphemer, unable to grasp the depth of my message or the love that fuels my mission.

Each accusation feels like a weight pressing down on my spirit. It wounds me to know that those who once walked with me, who witnessed miracles and felt my compassion, now fail to recognize the truth of my identity. I long to reach them, to share the light that shines within me, but their hearts are closed, blinded by fear and doubt.

In this moment, I reflect on my purpose and the love I have offered. Despite the pain of their rejection, I hold onto the hope that one day they will see, truly see, the love and grace that I embody. This suffering is part of my journey, and I must remain steadfast in my mission, even when my true self remains obscured in their eyes.

The accusations hurled at me—blasphemy and claiming to be the King of the Jews—feel like arrows aimed straight at my heart. Each charge is rooted in a fear that has taken hold of the religious leaders, stemming from their own insecurities and jealousy. They see me not as a messenger of God, but as a threat to their authority and influence. This realization weighs heavily on me, for I know that their motivations are clouded by a desperation to maintain control.

The role of the crowd becomes painfully clear as I take in the shifting sentiments around me. Faces that once reflected joy and hope have morphed into expressions of doubt and hostility. Initially, there were those who supported me, drawn by the miracles I performed and the teachings I shared. But as fear spreads through the crowd, their collective voice becomes a deafening chorus calling for my crucifixion. It's a heartbreaking transformation, illustrating how quickly faith can dissolve when faced with the unfamiliar. The dynamic of mob mentality is striking, revealing how easily people can be swayed by emotion rather than reason. The same individuals who once sang my praises now demand my demise, and it is chilling to witness how swiftly their loyalties shift under pressure.

As the trial unfolds, I cannot help but confront the misunderstandings that have led to this moment. My teachings, meant to illuminate the path to love, forgiveness, and radical humility, have been twisted into something menacing. I think of the parables I shared, intended to unveil deeper truths about God's kingdom, and how they have been reduced to mere words that incite fear instead of inspiring hope. The essence of my mission—to bring healing and liberation—has been obscured by the shadows of misinterpretation.

The people expected a political liberator, a warrior king who would overthrow their oppressors. They are unable to see that my call to love one another and serve with humility is not a threat, but a promise of true freedom. As I listen to their accusations, I am struck by the profound disconnect between my intentions and their expectations. In this moment, I wish I could convey the depth of my message, but their hearts are hardened, their ears closed by fear and misunderstanding.

As the trial continues, I remain resolute, knowing that the true depth of my mission transcends this moment. My silence in the face of these accusations will speak louder than any defense I could muster. In this painful experience, I hope to reveal the true nature of love and sacrifice, even when faced with injustice. Through this trial, I long to illuminate the ways in which fear can distort our understanding and lead us away from the truth, leaving a lasting impact on those who witness it.

The trial stands as a stark reflection of the injustice that permeates the world. Here, truth is overshadowed by fear, and the voices of the powerful drown out the cries for compassion. Accusations fly, not based on reality but on a desperate need to maintain control and power.

In this moment, I see how easily love can be twisted into hatred, how fear can blind even the most devoted hearts. The crowd, once filled with followers, now turns against me, illustrating the fragile nature of faith and understanding in the face of adversity.

This trial is not just a personal affront; it is a mirror showing the systemic injustices that plague humanity. It reveals the struggles of the marginalized, the pain of the oppressed, and the silence of those who could stand for truth but choose to remain quiet.

Yet, in this darkness, I hold onto hope. I see the potential for change, the possibility that even in moments of despair, love can break through. This injustice fuels my resolve to speak the truth, to embody compassion, and to inspire others to seek a world where love prevails over fear and understanding triumphs over division.

The manner in which the trial is conducted is a far cry from what justice demands. Witnesses are brought forth, but their testimonies are riddled with contradictions, and yet, they are accepted without scrutiny. I observe the hastiness with which decisions are made, as if the outcome is predetermined. There is no serious consideration of evidence or the validity of the accusations against me. Instead, the religious leaders appear more concerned with maintaining their authority and influence than with seeking the truth. It is a striking reflection of how power can corrupt, leading to a distortion of justice.

This trial is not merely a personal affront to me; it symbolizes a broader human tendency that has persisted throughout history. People often prioritize power and control over truth and righteousness, creating a climate where injustice thrives. The leaders who stand in judgment have lost sight of their original calling to guide and shepherd the people. Their actions betray a fear of losing their positions rather than a commitment to the well-being of the community. In their quest for self-preservation, they have sacrificed the very essence of their roles, demonstrating how the pursuit of power can blind even the most devout.

Suddenly another blow to the back of my neck.

As I regain my footing, the pain radiating from my back reminds me of the harshness of this journey. The crowd's murmurs blend into a cacophony of voices—some mocking, others sympathetic—but I focus on the strength rising within me. Each blow is a reminder of the weight of humanity's sins, and I carry it willingly, knowing it is part of a greater purpose.

I glance at the soldiers, their faces hardened by their roles, and I feel a pang of sorrow for them, too. They are caught in a cycle of violence and fear, just as many in the crowd are. In this moment of suffering, I am determined to show them that love can break through even the thickest walls of anger and despair.

With each step forward, I feel the burden of the cross but also the promise of hope. Despite the blows and the anguish, I am resolute. As with the trial, I will not let this moment define me; I will rise above it, embodying the love that transcends suffering. I press on, each step a declaration that even in the face of despair, hope endures.

In this moment, I am reminded of the weight of the prophecies that spoke of the suffering servant. The injustices I face are not merely incidental; they are part of a larger narrative that reveals humanity's struggle with truth. The betrayal of justice reflects a deep-seated fear within the human heart—the fear of change, of confronting the uncomfortable truths about oneself and the world. Those who should be my defenders have become my accusers, driven by a desire to protect their own interests rather than seeking the welfare of their people.

As the trial continues, I cannot help but reflect on the implications of this moment. It is a powerful reminder of the fragility of justice in the hands of those who prioritize their agendas over moral integrity. The crowd, swayed by fear and the allure of authority, becomes complicit in this injustice, showcasing the vulnerability of the human spirit when faced with uncertainty. This collective blindness to truth highlights the urgency of my mission—to awaken hearts to the power of love, compassion, and understanding.

The injustice I endure is a call to action for all who witness it. It compels me to stand firm in my purpose, to embody the very teachings I have shared: that true strength lies not in retaliation but in unwavering love. Even as the trial unfolds with all its failures, I resolve to respond not with anger or bitterness but with grace. My silence becomes a powerful statement, a testament to the strength of faith that transcends the immediate injustices I face.

In this painful crucible, I cling to the hope that, through my suffering, a greater truth will emerge—a truth that will challenge the very foundations of injustice and inspire future generations to seek righteousness over power. The trial is not just a personal struggle; it is a universal reflection of the human condition, a reminder that the pursuit of truth often comes at a great cost.

Pontius Pilate presents a striking figure, embodying the complexities of power and authority. He stands at an average height, but his posture is commanding, suggesting a man accustomed to exerting control. His physique is robust, reflecting a military background, with broad shoulders and a square jaw that conveys determination. Pilate's hair is dark, neatly groomed, though it shows traces of gray, hinting at the burdens of leadership and the weight of the decisions he faces.

His face is etched with lines that reveal the tension of his position—furrowed brows that hint at constant deliberation and a tightness around his mouth that betrays an inner conflict. His eyes are a deep brown, sharp and piercing, often shifting between an expression of authority and one of uncertainty. There's a flicker of apprehension in his gaze as he contemplates the choices before him, an awareness of the potential consequences of his actions.

Dressed in a Roman tunic, adorned with a breastplate that signifies his status, Pilate carries himself with an air of self-assuredness, yet there is an underlying vulnerability. The gold accents on his attire glint in the dim light of the trial chamber, symbolizing his rank while also serving as a reminder of the superficiality of power. His demeanor oscillates between that of a hardened governor and a man caught in a moral quagmire.

As he addresses those gathered in the trial, his voice resonates with authority but occasionally falters, revealing a hesitation that contrasts sharply with his outward composure. He speaks with a measured tone, attempting to maintain control over the proceedings, but there is an evident struggle as he navigates the tumultuous atmosphere created by the crowd's demands. In moments of tension, his fingers may twitch, betraying an anxiety that simmers beneath the surface, reflecting the burden of his authority in such a critical moment.

Pilate's expression shifts throughout the trial—moments of disdain when confronted with the accusations against me, flashes of sympathy as he grapples with the reality of my innocence, and hints of frustration when faced with the unyielding crowd. His demeanor captures the duality of his role: a ruler striving to maintain order, yet internally conflicted by the injustice unfolding before him.

I strain to stand upright. Simon whispers to me but I cannot hear him.

As I stand before him, I sense the internal conflict that churns within him. Here is a man caught between duty and morality, a leader grappling with the weight of public opinion and the stark reality of justice. Pilate's position is precarious; he is fully aware of my innocence, yet he remains trapped in a web of political maneuvering. His gaze flickers with uncertainty as he contemplates the choice before him: to uphold the truth or to bow to the pressure of the crowd clamoring for my condemnation.

Pilate's struggle embodies the complexities of leadership in times of crisis. The role of a ruler is not merely to enforce the law but to embody justice and righteousness. Yet here he stands, a man of power, caught in a moment where the scales of justice tip dangerously toward the whims of the mob. He questions me, probing for clarity, yet I can see that his heart is not fully in it. His attempts to deflect responsibility—sending me to Herod, hoping the situation will resolve itself—speak to a profound unwillingness to confront the truth directly. He seems to know that condemning me is wrong, but the fear of losing control, of inciting unrest among the people, overwhelms him.

The depths of Pilate's moral conflict resonate with me. His capitulation to public pressure reveals a painful truth about leadership: the potential for corruption when the desire for approval overrides the pursuit of justice. In a moment that should be defined by courage, Pilate chooses safety over righteousness, sacrificing the innocent to appease the masses. It is a stark reminder of how often the powerful have prioritized their interests at the expense of the vulnerable.

Judas! Where are you Judas?

As I reflect on my personal experience of injustice, I feel the weight of betrayal crushing my heart. To be wrongfully accused by those I have come to save is a pain deeper than I can articulate. I think of the countless lives I have touched, the hearts I have healed, and the love I have shared with my disciples. Yet here I am, standing before the very representatives of the people I sought to uplift, facing accusations rooted in fear and misunderstanding. The betrayal stings, not only because of the injustice itself but also because it reveals a profound disconnect between my mission and their perception of me.

In this moment, I confront the anguish of knowing that my teachings of love and forgiveness have been twisted into something unrecognizable. The faces in the crowd, once filled with hope and joy, now reflect anger and rejection. I wonder how many of them truly understand who I am and what I represent. This betrayal is not just personal; it encapsulates the broader human experience of misunderstanding, fear, and the struggle to see the truth amidst the noise.

Yet, even as the pain of betrayal lingers, I recognize that my path is not one of bitterness but of resolve. I feel the strength of my calling surging within me, urging me to embody the very principles I have preached. In the face of injustice, I am reminded that true power lies not in defending oneself but in standing firm in faith and purpose. As I look into Pilate's eyes, I see not just a judge but a reflection of humanity's struggle with fear and the choice between right and wrong.

Judas. Who are you Judas?

In the dim light of the trial, I find myself contemplating the profound nature of fear and how it can distort humanity's perception of truth. Fear has a powerful grip on the hearts and minds of the religious leaders and the crowd gathered before me. It breeds suspicion and leads to irrational decisions, often pushing individuals to reject what is right in favor of self-preservation and the maintenance of their own power. The religious leaders, threatened by my teachings and the growing influence I have over the people, succumb to their fear of losing their authority. Their motivations become clouded by a desperate need to protect their positions, even if it means condemning an innocent man.

As I observe the shifting expressions on the faces of the crowd, I see how fear has transformed their support into hostility. Initially drawn to my message of love and hope, they are now swayed by the panic instilled in them by their leaders. They grapple with the uncertainty of the future, and in their confusion, they lash out, choosing the familiar path of anger over the unsettling invitation to embrace compassion and understanding. This mob mentality, fueled by fear, illustrates how quickly humanity can turn against its own, choosing to cast aside empathy when confronted with the unknown.

My own heart aches at this profound misunderstanding. In a moment that should reflect the values of love and grace, fear has warped the narrative. I think of the core message I have shared throughout my ministry—the call to love one another, to forgive, and to stand for justice. Yet here we are, in a moment of great injustice, where those very values are cast aside in favor of preserving a fragile status quo. It's a painful reminder that fear often leads to actions that contradict the very essence of what it means to be human, to connect with one another in compassion and solidarity.

The irony is not lost on me: I stand accused of blasphemy and treason for proclaiming the truth that could set them free. Yet fear blinds them to the light I offer. In this tense atmosphere, I am reminded that humanity's struggle with fear is not new; it echoes through history, manifesting in various forms—be it the fear of change, fear of the other, or the fear of losing control. Each of these fears has the potential to ignite violence, rejection, and division. As I stand silent before my accusers, I ponder the challenge before me: how to transform fear into understanding, how to foster a community built on trust rather than suspicion.

More and more I now understand not only the frailty of human nature but also the urgent need for love and understanding to triumph over the shadows that fear casts. In this moment of trial, I seek to embody the very message I have preached—to remain steadfast in love and faith, even in the face of overwhelming misunderstanding.

Judas. Why?

As I stand before my accusers, I am acutely aware of the profound impact that misunderstanding has on humanity. It weaves through the fabric of society, creating rifts that divide individuals and communities, often rooted in fear and ignorance. I recall instances from my ministry where misunderstanding led to division among people who should have been united by a shared pursuit of truth and compassion. The very teachings that were meant to bring healing often became the catalyst for conflict.

For instance, when I spoke to the Samaritan woman at the well, my message of acceptance and love was met with skepticism and hostility from those who could not reconcile their beliefs with my actions. They viewed her as an outcast, unworthy of compassion, and in their misunderstanding, they failed to see the beauty of reconciliation that I sought to offer. Instead of embracing the opportunity for dialogue and growth, they chose to cling to their prejudices, perpetuating a cycle of division that has echoed through the ages.

Thoughts of Judas's betrayal echo in my head, a haunting reminder of trust shattered. The weight of his kiss lingers, a symbol of the ultimate treachery. I recall the moments we shared, the teachings exchanged, and the bond we forged. It stings deeply to know that someone so close to me chose to turn away, driven by greed and fear.

In this moment of trial, I feel a mixture of sorrow and compassion for him. His actions stem from a place of turmoil, and I can't help but wonder if he sees the path he has chosen. The betrayal cuts deep, but I refuse to let it consume me. Instead, I focus on the love that remains, the hope that persists despite the darkness.

As I face the consequences of our journey together, I hold onto the belief that even this betrayal can lead to redemption. I will not let the echoes of his choice define my mission; rather, I will transform this pain into a testament of grace, embodying the very love that Judas failed to understand.

The voice of Judas echo in my head: Because it must be so.

In this moment of trial, I am struck by how easily misunderstanding can lead to hostility. The religious leaders, consumed by their desire to maintain power, misinterpret my intentions, believing that my message threatens their authority. They fail to engage with the very essence of what I teach—love, forgiveness, and unity. Their inability to listen and consider differing perspectives blinds them to the possibility of a deeper truth. Instead of dialogue, they resort to accusations and condemnation, stoking the fires of animosity among the crowd.

As I observe the crowd, I see faces filled with confusion and anger. They have been led to believe that I am a threat, a blasphemer deserving of punishment. Their misunderstanding perpetuates hostility, turning supporters into adversaries, all because they cannot see beyond their fears and preconceived notions. The whispers of the religious leaders have sown seeds of doubt, and rather than seeking to understand my message, they lash out, choosing to believe the narrative that best serves their fears.

The consequences of this failure to truly listen and engage are staggering. Relationships fracture, communities splinter, and the opportunity for growth and understanding is lost. The irony is that I stand before them not as a foe, but as a friend—someone who has come to offer healing and hope. Yet their unwillingness to hear me only deepens the chasm between us.

Judas: It must be so.

In this moment of injustice, I reflect on the urgent need for humanity to embrace understanding as a core value. To truly listen to one another is to invite connection, to dismantle the barriers that division erects. Each interaction holds the potential to bridge gaps and foster compassion, yet misunderstanding often becomes the wall that keeps us apart. It is a painful reminder of the work that lies ahead—a call to encourage open hearts and minds, to challenge preconceived notions, and to seek the truth that resides in authentic dialogue.

As I prepare to face the consequences of this trial, I carry with me the weight of these reflections. I yearn for a world where love triumphs over misunderstanding, where the desire for connection outweighs the fear of the unknown. In these final moments, I resolve to embody that truth, even in the face of profound injustice. I will stand firm in my faith, demonstrating that love, compassion, and understanding are the only paths to true freedom.

Judas: It is as it should be.

In the face of fear and misunderstanding, the call to empathy becomes even more vital. As I reflect on the dynamics of the trial and the responses of those around me, I see how easily fear can cloud judgment, leading to actions that betray our values and humanity. It is in these moments of uncertainty that the ability to empathize with others can bridge divides and foster understanding.

Empathy requires us to step outside of ourselves, to momentarily set aside our fears and biases, and to genuinely seek to understand the experiences and emotions of others. When we cultivate empathy, we open ourselves to the possibility of connection, even with those who hold differing views. Empathy is not just a response; it is a practice, a commitment to nurturing understanding even when it feels challenging. In times of uncertainty, remember that your willingness to empathize can help dismantle barriers of misunderstanding. It can transform fear into compassion, hostility into connection. Each act of empathy has the power to ripple outward, influencing others and fostering a spirit of unity.

Judas: It cannot be otherwise.

In the face of relentless accusations and the chaotic atmosphere of the trial, I found a profound strength in silence. As I stood before my accusers, the weight of their words hung heavily in the air, a cacophony of fear and hostility directed at me. Yet, amidst this turmoil, I chose to remain composed, recognizing that sometimes the most powerful response is one of quiet resolve.

My silence was not born of weakness or defeat; rather, it was a deliberate act of strength. In a world that often equates noise with power, my decision to withhold a defensive outburst was a profound statement. It demonstrated that I did not need to engage in their accusations or justify myself against their falsehoods. In that moment, I embodied a resistance against the injustice unfolding before me—a testament to the belief that truth stands firm, even when not vocally defended.

There is a unique power in silence, one that can convey more than words ever could. It allows for reflection and contemplation, creating a space where deeper truths can resonate. In this charged environment, my silence spoke volumes about my commitment to my mission and the values I upheld. It was a refusal to be swept away by the fervor of the crowd or the manipulations of those in power.

Furthermore, my silent strength served as a mirror for those present. In the face of hostility, my calmness invited reflection among the onlookers, compelling them to confront the gravity of their actions. Silence can serve as a catalyst for introspection, prompting others to question their own beliefs and motivations. In a trial marked by misunderstanding and fear, my quiet composure became a beacon of steadfastness, reminding all who were present that true strength often lies in restraint.

This moment of silent strength resonates beyond the confines of the trial. It speaks to the heart of human experience, illustrating that there are times when the loudest voice is one that chooses not to speak. It reminds us that amidst chaos and accusations, we can find strength in composure and integrity.

Judas: It is your destiny.

During the trial, as I stood before my accusers and faced the relentless storm of accusations, my faith became my anchor. In the midst of chaos, it provided me with a profound sense of inner strength and clarity. Each moment felt like a tumultuous wave crashing against the shore, yet my unwavering belief in the Father's purpose held me steady.

My faith was not a mere abstraction; it was a living, breathing force that reminded me of my mission. I recalled the moments spent in prayer, where I sought guidance and strength from the Father. Those quiet conversations, often held in solitude, nurtured my spirit and solidified my resolve. As the trial unfolded, I drew upon those sacred moments, finding reassurance in the knowledge that I was fulfilling a divine plan, even in the face of such profound adversity.

Prayer became a vital lifeline amidst the turmoil. It was not merely a recitation of words but an intimate communion with the Father, a chance to share my burdens and seek comfort. Each breath, each whispered plea, brought me closer to the divine purpose that lay ahead. I was reminded of the path I had walked—the healings, the teachings, the love shared with my disciples—and this recollection fortified my heart against the weight of the present moment.

In my most trying times, I found clarity in my mission. My faith illuminated the path ahead, guiding my thoughts and actions even as falsehoods swirled around me. I knew that my suffering was not in vain; it was a necessary part of the larger narrative of redemption. This understanding brought a sense of peace, allowing me to navigate the complexities of the trial with unwavering focus.

Moreover, the connection with my Father imbued me with a sense of purpose that transcended the immediate pain and injustice. I understood that my response to this trial would resonate far beyond the confines of this moment, shaping the future for countless souls. In the depths of adversity, I felt a profound responsibility not only to uphold the truth but to embody the very love and compassion I had preached.

This experience served as a powerful reminder of the strength that faith can provide in our darkest hours. It underscores the importance of cultivating a deep relationship with the divine, one that sustains us when we confront challenges that seem insurmountable.

Judas: It is fated. Inescapable.

Standing firm in one's convictions during times of trial is a profound act of courage. As I faced the tumult of accusations and the pressure of the crowd, the significance of unwavering faith became crystal clear. It is in those moments of overwhelming opposition that the strength of one's beliefs is tested, revealing the true depth of our commitment to our values and our mission.

Standing firm meant embracing the truth of my teachings and the love I had shared with others, even when surrounded by hostility. It required not just inner resolve but also a willingness to bear witness to the message I had come to share—one of compassion, forgiveness, and redemption. This steadfastness was not merely about resisting external pressures; it was about embodying the principles that I had preached throughout my ministry.

The act of standing firm can often feel isolating, especially when the world around us seems to reject what we hold dear. Yet, it is precisely in those moments of isolation that we can draw strength from our convictions. I reflected on the countless teachings I had shared with my disciples, reminding them that true faith often involves sacrifice and endurance. The power of standing firm lies in its ability to inspire others, offering them a beacon of hope amidst uncertainty and fear.

Judas. Accept.

As the verdict rings out, a wave of emotions crashes over me—shock, sorrow, and a profound sense of inevitability. Hearing the crowd call for my crucifixion, I feel a deep ache in my heart for those who have turned against me, their judgment clouded by fear and misunderstanding.

Yet amid this turmoil, I am filled with a calm acceptance. I understand that this moment is part of a greater purpose, a necessary path toward redemption. I take a deep breath, grounding myself in the love I carry for all humanity, even for those who condemn me.

In this moment of injustice, I am resolute. I resolve to embody the teachings I have shared—to forgive, to love, and to demonstrate compassion, even in the face of cruelty. This verdict does not define me; it is merely a step in a journey that transcends my suffering.

I look out at the crowd, seeking connection even in their anger. I silently pray that one day they will understand the depth of my message and the love that fuels it. With a heavy heart but unwavering spirit, I prepare to walk the path laid before me, knowing that hope can rise even from the darkest moments.

Judas, I am sorry.

Chapter 9: The Crucifixion

As I arrive at Golgotha the starkness of the landscape looms before me. The hill, often referred to as the Place of the Skull, is desolate and foreboding, surrounded by a throng of spectators. The air is heavy with an unsettling mix of anticipation and dread. The crowd is a restless sea of faces, some filled with contempt, others steeped in sorrow, while a few stand in confused silence. Their murmurs create a dissonant backdrop, and the tension rises as the soldiers prepare for the grim proceedings ahead.

The preparations for the crucifixion are methodical yet chaotic. Soldiers move about with grim efficiency, their armor glinting in the harsh sunlight, gathering the instruments of my suffering. I can feel the weight of the wooden cross bearing down on my shoulders—its rough, splintered surface a painful reminder of the agony that awaits. The eyes of the crowd pierce through me, some casting scornful glares, while others look on with pity, their hearts heavy with the knowledge of what is to come. The atmosphere is thick with a sense of impending sorrow, as if the very earth holds its breath in anticipation of the pain that will soon unfold.

As I approach the cross, my thoughts drift back over the journey that led me here. I recall the countless miles traveled, the teachings shared, the miracles witnessed, and the relationships forged. Each step has been part of a divine narrative that now crescendos in this tragic yet pivotal moment. Memories of laughter and joy are overshadowed by the weight of betrayal and abandonment. My disciples, once so close, have scattered in fear, leaving me to face this trial alone. Yet, I cannot help but reflect on the love I hold for them and for all humanity, a love that fuels my resolve even in the face of unimaginable suffering.

The emotional toll of what lies ahead is almost suffocating. I know the physical pain I will endure, but it is the spiritual anguish that weighs heaviest upon my heart. I carry the burden of humanity's sin, the collective grief and darkness that has separated us from the Father. The agony of this moment is not merely about my impending death; it is about the love that compels me to embrace it. It is the ultimate act of sacrifice, a fulfillment of the promise made to humanity—a promise of redemption through suffering.

This moment is a culmination of all that I have sought to teach and embody. As I stand on the brink of crucifixion, I recognize that the profound significance of what will transpire is woven into the fabric of love itself. In this sacred hour, the depths of human pain and divine love will intersect in a way that will change the course of history forever.

The journey to the cross begins with the arrest in the Garden of Gethsemane, a moment steeped in betrayal and anguish. My closest companions, who once walked with me, are now fragmented by fear and confusion. As the soldiers approach, led by Judas, I feel the weight of their hostility, their intentions sharp and unforgiving. The kiss of betrayal stings more than any weapon; it shatters the bonds of love and trust that I held dear. Yet, even in this moment of deep sorrow, I choose to embrace the path laid before me, understanding that this suffering is integral to the fulfillment of my mission.

The trial that follows is a tumultuous whirlwind of accusations and scorn. I stand before the religious leaders and Pontius Pilate, bearing witness to the injustices of a system that values power over truth. As they hurl charges of blasphemy and treason, I remain composed, aware of the divine purpose unfolding. I feel the weight of the world's sin pressing upon my shoulders, a burden that is both heavy and humbling. In their eyes, I see not just the judgment of one man but the collective fear and misunderstanding of humanity.

The physical journey to Golgotha is arduous and grueling. The soldiers force me to carry the heavy wooden beam of the cross, its rough surface biting into my skin. Each step feels like an eternity, a reminder of the suffering that awaits. I stumble, my body weakened by the beatings and humiliation I've endured. The mocking shouts of the crowd echo in my ears, a cacophony of disdain and derision. Some jeer and ridicule, while others weep, their hearts torn by the sight of a man they once revered, now treated as a common criminal.

As I walk this path, I cannot help but reflect on the faces of those who have come to witness my crucifixion. There are familiar faces among the crowd—friends, disciples, and those whose lives I have touched. I see Mary, my mother, her eyes filled with anguish, and the sight of her pain pierces my heart. I long to comfort her, to ease her sorrow, but I know that this moment is not just about personal suffering; it is about something far greater. It is about love, sacrifice, and the promise of redemption.

The burden of the cross becomes a symbol of my own suffering and the suffering of humanity. Each step is a testament to the depth of love I carry, a love that compels me to endure the unthinkable. As the journey continues, I see the soldier's faces, hardened by duty, yet I sense a flicker of uncertainty in their eyes. They are instruments of this violence, yet their humanity remains. I wonder if they recognize the magnitude of what they are about to witness—the crucifixion of the Son of God.

Finally, we reach Golgotha, a place marked by sorrow and death. As I stand before the cross, I take a moment to breathe deeply, allowing the weight of this moment to wash over me. The preparation is grim; the soldiers ready the nails and hammer, indifferent to the life they are about to extinguish. In this final moment, I reflect on the love that has guided my every step, the love that has compelled me to walk this path of suffering.

The process of crucifixion is not merely a physical act; it embodies the depths of human despair and the unfathomable love of God. As the nails pierce my flesh, I know that my suffering is not in vain. It is the ultimate expression of love, a bridge between humanity and the divine. In this moment, I embrace my destiny, fully aware that this act will echo through the ages as a testament to the power of love and sacrifice.

As I hang on the cross, my thoughts begin to spiral, becoming less lucid with each passing moment. The pain radiates through my body, blurring the edges of my consciousness. I find myself lost in a haze, memories intertwining with the present, each recollection slipping away before I can grasp it fully.

The weight of my body pulls me deeper into this spiral. The agony is relentless, and I can feel my focus fading. I am aware of my drifting mind, the way thoughts flicker like a dying flame—first a memory of laughter, then the sting of betrayal. It's maddening, this loop of emotion and pain that intertwines, making it hard to find clarity.

I cling to the hope that my suffering serves a purpose, yet that thought, too, begins to twist and bend, losing its solidity. What is the meaning of this agony? I grasp for answers, but they elude me, swirling in a whirlwind of confusion.

In this fog of pain, I yearn for understanding, yet the clarity I seek slips further away. I am trapped in this moment, caught between despair and the flickering light of love I still believe in. Even as my mind becomes a tangled web, I hold onto the conviction that my sacrifice can bring forth hope, even if that truth feels increasingly distant.

As I hang on the cross, suspended between heaven and earth, a flood of emotions washes over me. The physical pain is excruciating, yet it is the emotional and spiritual toll that weighs most heavily on my heart. In this moment, I reflect on the nature of suffering—not just my own, but the suffering of all humanity. Every pain, every sorrow, every injustice that has ever been endured resonates within me. I bear not only the weight of my own anguish but the burdens of countless souls who have cried out in desperation and despair.

Suffering has many faces; it can be a silent ache in the heart or a loud cry of anguish. In my own suffering, I recognize the depth of human experience—the loneliness that accompanies pain, the feelings of abandonment, and the struggle to find meaning in the midst of turmoil. I recall the times when others have suffered—those who came to me seeking healing, the broken-hearted, the marginalized. Their stories weave together a tapestry of shared humanity, reminding me that suffering is a universal experience, one that connects us all.

In this moment of agony, I embrace the transformative power of suffering. It is through pain that we often discover our deepest strengths, our greatest compassion, and our most profound love. The very act of enduring this crucifixion is a testament to the resilience of the human spirit. Even as my body cries out in agony, my heart swells with love for those who have walked alongside me, who have believed in me, and who will carry my message forward. This suffering is not just an end; it is a beginning, a catalyst for change and healing.

The words of the prophets echo in my mind as I ponder the significance of this moment. I remember how they spoke of suffering as a path to redemption, a way to bring about transformation. My own suffering now embodies that prophecy. I think of those who will come after me—who will face their own trials and tribulations. I want them to know that suffering does not define them; rather, it can refine them, shaping their character and drawing them closer to one another and to God.

As the pain intensifies, I find solace in the thought of forgiveness. The very purpose of this crucifixion is rooted in love and the desire to reconcile humanity with the Father. I am here to extend grace, even in my final moments. I reflect on the many times I have preached about forgiveness—how it is a release, a letting go of the burdens we carry. In my heart, I resolve to embody that message even now. My suffering must lead to forgiveness, for it is through forgiveness that true healing can occur.

With every agonizing breath, I focus on those who stand at the foot of the cross—my beloved disciples, the women who have followed me, and even the onlookers who have come to witness this moment. Their faces reflect a mix of sorrow, confusion, and heartbreak. I wish to reassure them, to instill hope amid despair. My heart aches for them, knowing the depth of their love and their pain in witnessing this sacrifice.

I am reminded that love is not just an emotion; it is an action, a choice made even in the face of suffering. I commit to demonstrating this love until my final breath, knowing it will reverberate through time and inspire those who witness it. I am here to show that love triumphs over suffering and that through this act, humanity will find a path to healing.

As I continue to endure the physical pain, my spirit remains resolute. I find strength in the knowledge that this moment, however agonizing, serves a greater purpose. It is an expression of divine love, one that will transcend the boundaries of time and space. My suffering is a bridge—a way to connect the divine with the human, to offer hope where there is despair.

In this crucible of pain, I hold fast to the truth that love and suffering are intertwined. They exist in a delicate dance, each giving meaning to the other. It is in this suffering that I find my identity, my mission, and my ultimate purpose. I am here to demonstrate that love persists, even in the darkest moments, and that it is this love that will ultimately redeem the world.

The agony intensifies, but amidst the pain, I find clarity. I think of the many who have wronged me, the betrayal I have faced, and the misunderstanding that has led to this moment. It would be easy to succumb to anger or despair, but I choose a different path. I understand the transformative power of forgiveness, not just for those who seek it, but for myself as well.

As I hang on the cross, my thoughts begin to fade faster, slipping through my grasp like grains of sand. The pain is overwhelming, a relentless tide that pulls me under, drowning my clarity. Each breath comes with a struggle, and the edges of my awareness blur into a haze of confusion.

Memories. I try to hold onto them, to find strength in their warmth, but the effort becomes exhausting. The loop of my thoughts tightens, each idea spiraling back to pain and betrayal, and I feel myself sinking deeper into the darkness.

I am aware of my drifting mind, the way my focus slips away, like a candle flickering in a storm. I search for meaning in this suffering, but the questions swirl around me without resolution. What is the purpose of this agony? Is there hope in this darkness? These thoughts, once clear, now dissolve into a fog of uncertainty.

The crowd's voices blur into a distant murmur, their faces becoming indistinct shadows. I cling to the fragments of love that still resonate within me, but even they feel fleeting. As my thoughts fade, I find solace in the quiet acceptance of my fate. This suffering, though profound, is part of something greater—an echo of the love I strive to share.

And in this dimming consciousness, I hold onto that flicker of hope, even as it grows ever fainter, a final whisper amidst the chaos.

With great effort, I gather my strength and focus on the crowd below. I see faces filled with scorn, yet I also catch glimpses of love and compassion among my followers. The weight of my mission presses down upon me, and I realize that my suffering is not merely for myself—it is for all of humanity. In this moment, I am called to offer forgiveness, to break the cycle of pain and retribution that so often defines human interactions.

In a voice that struggles to carry over the tumult, I utter the words, "Father, forgive them, for they know not what they do." It is a declaration of love, a commitment to release the burdens of sin and misunderstanding. This is my gift to the world: the promise of forgiveness, even in the face of betrayal. I feel the power of those words resonating in the very core of my being. They encapsulate the essence of my teachings, the core of my message to humanity.

Forgiveness is not simply an act; it is a radical choice to let go of resentment and embrace love. I know that this will not be easy for those who have wronged me or for those who witness this act of grace. Yet, in this moment, I choose to embody the very essence of compassion. I recognize that many of those who have turned against me are acting out of fear, misunderstanding, and societal pressure. My heart aches for them, for they are trapped in a cycle of violence that they cannot see.

As I offer forgiveness, I also reflect on the burden of suffering that all of humanity carries. Each person has their own struggles, their own pain, and their own need for redemption. I see their faces, etched with lines of sorrow and fear, and I realize that we are all interconnected in our suffering. This crucifixion, while deeply personal, is also a collective experience. It speaks to the struggles of all who feel lost, abandoned, or unloved.

In this moment of utter vulnerability, I embrace the reality that forgiveness has the power to heal. It is not a sign of weakness; it is a testament to strength and resilience. By forgiving, I dismantle the walls that divide us, creating space for understanding and compassion to flourish. I wish to convey to all who witness this moment that love can overcome even the deepest wounds.

I am aware of the enormity of what I am offering. This act of forgiveness will ripple through time, challenging future generations to embrace the radical call to love one another, even in the face of betrayal. I hope that those who hear my words will take them to heart, understanding that forgiveness is a gift we give not only to others but also to ourselves.

This moment becomes a profound teaching for all who witness it. I want them to see that even in the depths of despair, love remains a powerful force. I am demonstrating that forgiveness is possible, even when faced with unimaginable pain. It is a choice that can lead to healing and transformation.

As I offer this forgiveness, I feel a sense of peace wash over me. I know that this moment, this choice, will forever alter the trajectory of humanity. Through my suffering, I am paving the way for a deeper understanding of love, grace, and compassion. This act of forgiveness is my final testament—a powerful reminder that even in the darkest times, love prevails, and it is through love that we find our true selves.

As I hang on the cross, I struggle to remain lucid, but the effort becomes increasingly difficult. Each wave of pain washes over me, pulling my thoughts deeper into a murky haze. I focus on the faces in the crowd, trying to find clarity in their expressions, but they blur together like shadows in a dream.

I grasp at memories, the teachings I shared, the moments of joy and connection. I want to hold onto these thoughts, to find strength in them, but they slip away like water through my fingers. It frustrates me to feel my mind fraying, my awareness dimming just when I need it most.

I remind myself to breathe, to stay present, yet the agony overwhelms me. I can feel the edges of my consciousness drifting, thoughts circling back on themselves, each question echoing without resolution. What does this all mean? Is there hope beyond this suffering? Each attempt to find answers leaves me more disoriented.

In this struggle, I feel a profound loneliness, the weight of my sacrifice pressing down not just on my body but on my spirit. I yearn for clarity, for understanding, yet the effort to maintain my focus becomes a battle I fear I might lose.

I cling to the fragments of love that still flicker within me, desperate to keep them alive even as everything else fades. With each heartbeat, I fight against the darkness encroaching on my mind, knowing that even in this agony, the message of love and redemption must endure.

The scene around me unfolds like a tapestry woven with a spectrum of human emotion. The crowd, a mass of faces and voices, reflects the complexity of the human spirit. Some stand with scornful expressions, their jeers cutting through the air like daggers, while others weep silently, mourning the unfolding tragedy. This juxtaposition of reactions reveals profound truths about humanity's capacity for both compassion and indifference.

I see the soldiers, hardened by their duties, treating this moment with an unsettling casualness. They divide my garments among themselves, casting lots without a second thought, completely oblivious to the sacredness of the moment. Their laughter and banter echo mockingly, a stark contrast to the gravity of my sacrifice. In their eyes, I am merely a nuisance, a criminal deserving of punishment, stripped of my humanity. Their indifference weighs heavily on my heart, for they embody the detachment that often arises when people distance themselves from the suffering of others.

Yet, amidst the scorn, there are those who stand in quiet sorrow. I notice a group of women, their faces etched with pain, tears streaming down their cheeks. They embody the compassion that seems to elude so many in the crowd. Their hearts ache not only for me but for the world that continues to spiral into violence and misunderstanding. In their grief, they express a profound connection to my mission—a recognition of the love I have shared and the hope I have offered. Their mourning is a reminder that love often finds its voice in silence, and their presence speaks volumes.

As I observe the mixed reactions, I am reminded of the teachings I shared during my ministry. I recall the parables of compassion, the call to love one's neighbor, and the importance of recognizing the humanity in everyone. The crowd embodies both the best and worst of humanity—those who choose empathy and those who turn away. Their diverse responses highlight the ongoing struggle between compassion and indifference that defines the human experience.

I think of how easy it is for people to become entrenched in their beliefs, to allow fear and prejudice to cloud their judgment. The jeers of the crowd stem from a place of misunderstanding—a fear of what they do not comprehend. They have failed to see the message of love I have preached; instead, they cling to their preconceived notions of power and control. In contrast, those who mourn reveal the power of vulnerability and the strength found in empathy. They remind me that there is always a choice to respond with love, even in the face of hatred.

This moment serves as a stark reflection of society's tendency to polarize. Some will choose to side with power, dismissing the marginalized and oppressed, while others will step forward in solidarity, recognizing the shared humanity that binds us all. I realize that my suffering is not merely personal; it is a reflection of the struggles faced by those who stand for justice, love, and compassion in a world that often chooses fear.

The division among the crowd mirrors the broader societal rifts that have existed throughout history. I hope that those who witness this moment will learn from it—that they will recognize the importance of standing against injustice and speaking out against indifference. Compassion is a powerful antidote to the cruelty of the world, and it is a choice that each individual must make. In this moment of despair, I desire for my sacrifice to inspire a shift in perspective, urging people to look beyond themselves and see the suffering of others.

As I hang on the cross, I feel myself slipping in and out of consciousness, each moment a fragile thread pulling me between clarity and darkness. The pain is a constant companion, gnawing at me, threatening to pull me under completely.

One moment, I am aware of the crowd—faces contorted with scorn and sorrow, their voices rising and falling like a distant tide. I want to reach out, to connect with those who still believe, but the effort feels monumental. The next moment, I am enveloped in a fog, memories flashing by—laughter, warmth, the gentle touch of hands healed by love.

I cling to these moments, but they are fleeting, dissolving into shadows as my mind drifts further away. I struggle to hold onto the thread of my thoughts, but each breath is a battle, and the weight of my body grows heavier. I can feel my consciousness wavering, slipping through my fingers like sand.

In these fragmented moments, I experience flashes of clarity, where the purpose of my sacrifice seems to rise to the surface. But just as quickly, those thoughts fade, replaced by a relentless tide of pain and confusion.

I long for understanding, for the strength to embody the love I've preached, even as everything around me becomes less distinct. The darkness beckons, yet I fight to remain present, hoping that even in this struggle, the message of hope and redemption will endure beyond my fading consciousness.

As I draw my last breaths, I carry the weight of these contrasting emotions with me. I hope that those who witness my final moments will be moved to reflect on their own lives and the choices they make. Will they stand in solidarity with the oppressed, or will they turn a blind eye to suffering? The lesson lies not only in my crucifixion but also in their responses to it.

In the cacophony of reactions, I cling to the knowledge that love has the power to transform. Even among those who jeer, there is the potential for awakening—an opportunity for them to realize the depth of their misunderstanding and to choose a different path. My hope is that the sorrow expressed by the mourners will resonate deeply within the hearts of those who have turned away from love, prompting a change in perspective that could ripple through generations.

As I hang there, I embrace the duality of this moment—the pain of betrayal and the beauty of compassion. I know that my final act will not be in vain; it will serve as a catalyst for change, a reminder that love must prevail over hatred, and that every choice we make carries weight. The crucifixion becomes not just a moment of suffering but a testament to the enduring power of love, even in the face of overwhelming adversity.

Every breath now becomes a painful reminder of the suffering that encompasses not only my body but also the human experience. In this moment, I find myself reflecting deeply on the nature of suffering—what it means to endure, to ache, and to confront the darkest parts of existence. Suffering is an integral part of life, one that shapes our souls and our understanding of love. It is a teacher, albeit a harsh one, revealing truths that joy cannot convey.

Understanding suffering requires a willingness to look beyond the surface. It is all too easy to see it as merely an affliction, a burden to be borne in silence. Yet, in the depths of suffering lies the potential for profound growth. I have witnessed how pain can forge resilience, prompting individuals to rise from the ashes of despair and emerge stronger. The very act of facing suffering head-on can awaken empathy within us, allowing us to connect with others in ways we never thought possible. Through shared suffering, we find common ground; we understand that we are not alone in our struggles. It creates a bond that transcends the superficial, a testament to the human spirit's tenacity.

As I consider my suffering in these final moments, I recognize that it serves a greater purpose. My crucifixion is not simply an end but a transformative act for humanity. It embodies the redemptive power of love, illustrating how profound sacrifice can pave the way for healing and reconciliation. I reflect on the teachings I shared during my ministry—the importance of loving one's neighbor, of showing compassion to the marginalized. Each lesson has led to this moment, where the weight of the world's sin rests upon my shoulders. In this suffering, I am offering humanity a path back to grace, a bridge over the chasm created by disobedience and separation from God.

My suffering connects intimately with the broader narrative of God's love—a love that willingly embraces pain for the sake of others. This moment fulfills the prophecies spoken long before my arrival, echoing through the ages and revealing the divine plan woven into the fabric of history. Each lash of the whip, each nail driven into my hands, is a part of that plan. In this act of self-sacrifice, I am embodying the ultimate expression of love: to lay down one’s life for one’s friends. It is a love that challenges the very essence of power and control, a love that chooses vulnerability over dominance.

In contemplating my suffering, I am reminded of the many faces I have encountered along my journey—those who suffer from illness, betrayal, loss, and despair. Each person I have met has carried their own cross, their own burden of pain. I have sought to alleviate their suffering, to offer hope and healing in the midst of their trials. Now, as I face my own suffering, I can see how it mirrors theirs. It connects us in a shared experience that transcends time and space. I endure not only for my own sake but for the sake of every soul that has ever known anguish.

As I reflect on this painful journey, I also recognize the transformative power that suffering holds. It strips away the facades we often wear, exposing our true selves. In moments of suffering, we confront our vulnerabilities, and in that confrontation, we often find clarity. I think of the many times I spoke of the need for humility and the importance of serving others. My own suffering lays bare the essence of these teachings, reminding me that love is often found in the most unlikely places—in the willingness to suffer alongside another, to share in their pain and to offer a hand of support.

In this crucible of suffering, I am drawn to the understanding that true love is not without its trials. To love deeply often requires us to endure hardship, to bear the weight of another's pain. My crucifixion serves as the ultimate testament to this truth—a love that persists even in the face of profound suffering. It invites all who witness it to embrace their own suffering, to recognize that it can lead to a deeper understanding of compassion, grace, and connection.

I remember the moments of love I shared with my disciples and the countless individuals I encountered during my ministry. Each encounter has been a thread woven into the tapestry of my life, forming a picture of love that endures beyond pain. It is a love that invites others into the fold, a love that extends grace to those who may feel unworthy. Through my suffering, I hope to inspire them to see that even in their darkest moments, love remains a guiding light—a force that can transform despair into hope.

As I hang on the cross, I close my eyes, desperately trying to remember moments of love. In the midst of my agony, those memories feel like lifelines, pulling me back from the brink of despair. I think of the warmth of a child's laughter, the joy of healing a broken heart, and the quiet moments shared with my disciples around the fire, filled with stories and dreams.

I remember the faces of those I've touched—the woman at the well, the lepers who were restored, the friends who stood by me in faith. Each memory flickers in my mind, illuminating the darkness that surrounds me. They remind me of the love that transcends suffering, of the hope I have shared with others.

But just as quickly, these cherished moments begin to blur, slipping away as pain threatens to overwhelm me. I grasp at them, willing them to stay, but the effort

feels exhausting. I remind myself that these connections, this love, is what gives my suffering meaning.
Even as I drift in and out of consciousness, I hold onto the belief that love can prevail, that my sacrifice will not be in vain. I focus on those memories, letting them fill me with warmth and strength, knowing they are the essence of my journey. With each heartbeat, I cling to the hope that love can endure, even in the face of darkness.
As I draw nearer to the end of my earthly journey, I am filled with a profound sense of purpose. My suffering is not in vain; it is a conduit for the love I wish to impart to humanity. It invites all to reflect on their own journeys and the suffering they may face. In embracing their pain, they can discover the strength to rise above it, to find hope amidst the despair.
In this moment of suffering, I affirm the profound truth that love and suffering are intertwined. My crucifixion will resonate through the ages, not merely as an event of anguish but as a testament to the boundless love of God. It is a love that meets us in our pain, that walks alongside us in our darkest hours, and that ultimately leads us to redemption. As I suffer, I do so with the hope that humanity will come to understand the depth of this love and the transformative power it holds.
But the emotional toll weighs heavily upon my heart. It is not merely the physical pain that pierces me, but the profound sense of betrayal and abandonment that echoes within. I recall the faces of those I loved, the disciples who walked alongside me, and the crowds that once celebrated my presence. Now, as I hang here, I feel their absence acutely, the silence of their support a haunting reminder of the distance that has grown between us.
Betrayal cuts deeper than any wound. It is a knife that twists in the heart, leaving scars that linger long after the act itself. I feel the sting of Judas's kiss, the very symbol of trust turned to treachery. How can one so close to me, one who shared in my mission and my love, choose to turn away? In this moment, I grapple with the pain of that choice, the weight of his actions bearing down on me as much as the nails through my hands and feet. Each breath I take is laced with the bitterness of betrayal, a reminder of the fragility of trust.
Alongside this betrayal comes a deep sense of abandonment. The disciples, who promised to stand by me, have fled in fear. I am alone, surrounded by a crowd that jeers and mocks. Their disdain cuts through the air like a whip, echoing the

doubts that have risen in the hearts of those who once believed in my message of love and hope. I feel the emotional ache of their abandonment, as if each of them has chosen to walk away from the very truth I sought to share.

In this crucible of pain, I also confront the weight of human sin. As I bear the cross, I am acutely aware that it is not merely my own suffering I endure; it is the collective anguish of humanity. Every sin, every act of selfishness and cruelty, weighs heavy on my heart. I am reminded that this moment is not just about my suffering—it is about the redemption of all who have ever wandered from the path of love. I carry their burdens, their pain, as I willingly take on the role of the sacrificial lamb.

Yet, even in the depths of this emotional turmoil, there remains a wellspring of love that flows through me. I look out upon the crowd, witnessing their ignorance and fear, and my heart aches not for myself, but for them. How tragic it is that they do not understand the magnitude of this moment, that they cannot see the love that drives me to this cross. I forgive them in my heart, knowing that their actions stem from misunderstanding and fear. They do not realize the depth of my love for them, a love that compels me to endure this suffering for their sake.

As I hang on the cross, the pain is overwhelming, yet in the depths of my suffering, I remember that suffering itself can be an act of love. Each moment of agony transforms into a testament of compassion, a reminder of the sacrifice made for the sake of others. I think of the countless lives I've touched, the healings I've performed, and the messages of hope I've shared.

This suffering is not without purpose; it is woven into the fabric of love. It is a path that can lead to redemption, both for myself and for those who witness it. I recall the moments spent with my disciples, teaching them about love, forgiveness, and the importance of bearing one another's burdens.

Even now, as I endure this crucible, I understand that my pain echoes the struggles of humanity. It connects me to every heart that has felt despair, every soul that has longed for hope. In this realization, I find a flicker of strength.

I embrace this suffering, not as a defeat, but as a profound expression of love. I am reminded that true love often involves sacrifice, that it can manifest in the willingness to endure for the sake of others. In this final act, I strive to embody that love, knowing that even in my darkest hour, I can illuminate the path for others.

I am reminded that suffering can also be a catalyst for change. It can inspire others to look beyond themselves, to see the suffering of their neighbors, and to respond with compassion. I hope that in my final moments, I can convey a message that transcends pain—a message that calls forth love in the face of hatred, understanding in the midst of fear.

In this moment of anguish, I am not defeated. Rather, I stand firm in the love that defines my mission. My suffering serves as a testament to that love, a love that endures all trials and tribulations. I invite humanity to witness this moment, to recognize the depths of compassion that flow from the cross. It is a call to embrace the love that can heal, the forgiveness that can mend broken relationships, and the strength that can arise even in the face of unimaginable suffering.

As the pain radiates through my body, a profound theme begins to emerge from the depths of my suffering: forgiveness. In this moment of anguish, I reflect on the concept of forgiveness itself—what it means to extend grace in the face of deep injustice and the human tendency to harbor resentment. The very essence of my mission has been to show the world the power of love, and forgiveness is perhaps its highest expression.

Forgiveness is not merely an act of relinquishing blame; it is a radical choice that challenges our instincts for retribution and self-preservation. It requires a strength that often feels beyond reach, especially when confronted with betrayal and cruelty. Yet, in this painful crucible, I am reminded that forgiveness reflects the very nature of God's love—unconditional, transformative, and boundless. As I bear the weight of the cross, I find that my ability to forgive those who have wronged me is a testament to the depth of that love. It is a love that transcends human frailty and speaks to the possibility of redemption for all.

I think of those who have driven the nails into my hands and feet—those who have mocked and jeered. My heart aches not for myself, but for them. They do not realize the gravity of their actions, nor do they understand the profound love that motivates my sacrifice. This realization brings clarity: my willingness to forgive them is not only an act of compassion; it is a means of connecting with the essence of what it means to be human.

As I utter the words, "Father, forgive them, for they do not know what they are doing," I encapsulate the spirit of forgiveness that I wish to extend. In these words, I am not merely excusing their actions; I am inviting divine grace into the midst of cruelty. This statement echoes the very heart of my teachings—that forgiveness is essential for healing and redemption. It is an acknowledgment of human fallibility, a reminder that we are all capable of misunderstanding and misjudgment. In offering forgiveness, I not only release them from the burden of their sin; I also affirm the possibility of transformation.

The significance of this moment cannot be overstated. It reveals the depths of love that I embody, a love that chooses to heal rather than to retaliate. Forgiveness becomes a powerful force, one that can break the chains of anger and bitterness. In this crucifixion, I am providing a model for humanity—a blueprint for how to navigate the complexities of relationships and the pain that often accompanies them.

As I hang on the cross, the pain is a constant reminder of my sacrifice, yet amidst the agony, I remember the transformative power of forgiveness. Each breath I take is heavy with the weight of what I endure, but my thoughts drift to the countless moments where love and forgiveness changed lives.

I think of the woman caught in sin, how I offered her compassion instead of condemnation. In that moment, I witnessed her transformation—a shift from shame to hope. I recall the prodigal son, welcomed back with open arms, a testament to the healing power of forgiveness in the hearts of those who stray.

Even now, I realize that this suffering can also be a source of forgiveness. I can offer grace to those who have turned against me, those who have betrayed and condemned me. In my heart, I feel a deep urge to forgive them, to release the weight of anger and hurt. It is in this act of forgiveness that I find strength, a way to break the cycle of pain that binds us all.

Forgiveness is not weakness; it is a radical act of love. It holds the power to heal not just the one who receives it, but also the one who gives. As I hang here, I choose to embrace that power, understanding that even in this darkest hour, I can still extend love to the world.

With each thought of forgiveness, I draw closer to the essence of my mission: to embody love, even amidst suffering, and to illuminate the path toward redemption for all.

As I reflect on the transformative power of forgiveness, I recognize that it serves as a healing balm for both the forgiver and the forgiven. When we choose to forgive, we are not only extending grace to others; we are freeing ourselves from the shackles of resentment and hurt. It is an act that can restore hope, even in the darkest of circumstances. The weight of unforgiveness can be suffocating, while the act of letting go opens up pathways to peace and reconciliation.

In these final moments, I hope that my example will inspire a profound shift in hearts and minds. Forgiveness is not an easy path, but it is one that leads to true freedom. It calls us to confront our pain, to acknowledge our humanity, and to reach for a love that transcends our limitations. In this act of forgiveness on the cross, I offer a glimpse into the redemptive power of love, urging all to recognize its potential to heal even the deepest wounds.

In choosing to forgive, I embody the very message I have sought to impart throughout my ministry—a message that calls forth the best in humanity, even when confronted with the worst. I hope that all who hear my words will come to understand that love, manifested through forgiveness, has the power to transform not only individual lives but the world itself. As I prepare to draw my last breath, I do so with the hope that this lesson will resonate, echoing through the ages as a testament to the enduring power of love and the divine capacity for forgiveness.

As I hang on the cross, the world around me seems to fade into a haze of pain and sorrow. The air is thick with tension, and the crowd's murmur blends into an indistinguishable sound of anguish and mockery. In this moment, every breath is a struggle, yet I am acutely aware of the significance of the words I am about to utter. The crucifixion, with all its brutality, serves as the backdrop for my final messages—each one laden with meaning, purpose, and love.

These words do not come from me. There is a much higher Essence present.

"It is finished." I declare.

Each syllable carries the culmination of my journey, the essence of my sacrifice, the end of my physical suffering, the fulfillment of a promise—a promise of redemption and hope for all humanity. With this realization, I embrace the depth of my sacrifice. "It is finished" becomes a declaration of hope, a promise that love endures beyond suffering, transcending even death itself. In this moment, I am at peace, knowing that my mission has been fulfilled, and the light of love will continue to shine in the hearts of those who believe.

"It is finished" is not the end; it is the beginning.

"My God, my God, why have you forsaken me?"

In this, the deepest moment of my agony, I feel an overwhelming sense of abandonment. The weight of my suffering presses down on me, and I grapple with the silence and despair that surrounds my plea. But even as I express this anguish, I know that my cry is not just one of despair; it is a call for understanding. I am affirming that it is okay to feel pain, to question, and to seek solace. My suffering is not in vain; it serves as a reminder that even in our darkest hours, we can reach out for hope and connection.

I take a breath, feeling the weight of those words. Though I feel forsaken by Man, I know that I am not forsaken by God.

These.

My final words.

An invitation to you.

An invitation to witness the depths of divine love.

An invitation to see the connection between suffering and divine love.

Chapter 10: Legacy; The Resurrection

In my final moments on the cross, a profound stillness surrounds me. The weight of my body hangs heavily, each breath a labor of love and sacrifice. Pain radiates through me, but amid this agony, I find a serene acceptance. I look out at the crowd—faces etched with sorrow and confusion, some still mocking, others weeping.

With what strength I have left, I gather my thoughts and speak my last words: "Father, into your hands I commit my spirit." In those words, I feel the depth of my faith and surrender, a testament to the connection I have maintained despite the suffering. As I release myself fully, I embrace the culmination of my mission.

As I exhale for the final time, a sense of peace washes over me. The weight of the world's sins, the burdens of betrayal and abandonment, all come together in this moment of release. My heart, though heavy, is filled with love—for those who have wronged me, for those who mourn, for all of humanity.

In this instant, I feel the sky darken, the earth tremble, and the very fabric of reality shift. I know that my sacrifice will echo through the ages, a testament that even in death, love prevails.

With my final earthly breath, I embody the hope of resurrection, a promise that suffering does not have the final word. As I relinquish my spirit, I leave behind a legacy of love and redemption, forever changing the hearts of those who believe. In this sacred moment, I transcend pain and death, becoming a light that will guide humanity through the darkness.

Yet the end is not final. As I linger in the liminal space between physical death and spiritual ascent, I reflect on the themes of my earthly journey—love, sacrifice, and redemption. My heart swells with urgency, for I know the importance of the message I must share. The weight of my experiences presses upon me, and I yearn to reach those who have walked alongside me, to impart the lessons learned through suffering and joy.

In this sacred moment, I see Mary Magdalene approaching, her heart heavy with grief. I feel her pain and longing, and as I call her name, "Mary," I see the flicker of recognition in her eyes. She rushes to me, disbelief and joy mingling in her embrace. I urge her, “Do not cling to me, for there is work to be done. Go, tell my brothers that I am alive. Share the news of hope!”

Then I appear to my disciples, who are gathered in fear and confusion. Their faces reflect the shadows of doubt, but I am here to dispel that darkness. “Peace be with you,” I say, my voice steady and full of love. They need to understand that my resurrection is not merely an event; it is a transformative promise for all humanity. “As the Father has sent me, so I am sending you,” I declare, igniting the fire of their mission.

Every word I share carries the weight of urgency. The world needs to know that love conquers all, that even in the face of death, hope endures. I urge them to go forth, to spread the message of grace and forgiveness. They must be the bearers of this light, igniting hearts with the truth that redemption is possible.

In these fleeting moments, I understand that my time on earth may have ended, but my spirit will live on through them. The seeds of love I have sown must blossom in the hearts of those who believe. I implore them to carry my message to the ends of the earth, to be the voices of compassion in a world that desperately needs it.

As I prepare to ascend to the spirit realm, I feel a profound sense of peace. My journey has come full circle, but the mission continues. Love will always be the answer, and through my followers, it will spread like wildfire, igniting hope in every corner of the world.

In the silence of my final moments, I reflect on the journey that has led from the crucifixion to the resurrection, I am acutely aware of the emotional weight this moment carries. My earthly death has filled many with despair and confusion. Yet, my resurrection stands as the ultimate affirmation of hope, a transformative event that redefines despair into promise. It is within this profound context that I wish to contemplate the legacy I leave behind—the teachings, the love shared, and the call to action for future generations.

Standing here, I feel a deep sense of responsibility. My life and the message I have shared resonate through time, and I hope they will inspire those who come after me. The journey has not been solely about the miracles, the healings, or the parables; it is also about the essence of love, faith, and compassion. These core principles are what I wish to embed in the hearts of those who will carry my message forward. It is love that binds humanity, faith that sustains in adversity, and compassion that calls us to serve one another.

I envision a future where my message serves as a beacon of light—a guiding principle that shapes interactions and nurtures communities. It is my hope that love will be recognized not merely as an emotion but as a powerful force for change. In a world often marred by division and strife, I yearn for future generations to understand that love is the antidote to hatred, a unifying thread that can heal wounds and mend broken relationships.

I also desire for my teachings on faith to encourage individuals to seek deeper connections, not only with the divine but also with one another. Faith is a source of strength, enabling people to navigate life's challenges with resilience and courage. I hope that those who hear my words will embrace faith as a guiding light in their lives, empowering them to make choices rooted in love and kindness.

Moreover, I implore future generations to cultivate compassion. In a time when the world is rife with suffering and injustice, the ability to empathize with others and respond with kindness is vital. Compassion has the power to transform lives, bridging divides and fostering understanding. I envision a world where acts of compassion are not merely responses to suffering but proactive efforts to uplift and support one another.

As I stand on the cusp of eternity, my thoughts turn to the profound impact I hope my life will have. I wish for my message to transcend time, encouraging individuals to be agents of love and compassion in their communities. I yearn for future generations to recognize that each act of kindness, no matter how small, contributes to a larger tapestry of hope and healing.

This legacy is not merely about what I have done; it is about what can be achieved through the love, faith, and compassion that I have sought to embody. I long for my message to inspire a movement of unity—a collective effort to create a world where all people are valued and loved, regardless of their backgrounds or beliefs.

As we embark on this exploration of my legacy, I invite you to reflect on the power of love, the strength found in faith, and the importance of compassion. These are the gifts I hope to leave behind, and my earnest prayer is that they will take root in the hearts of many, igniting a flame of hope and transforming the world for generations to come.

Love, at its core, is the essence of my teachings—a profound and transformative force that binds humanity together. It is a theme woven throughout my ministry, manifesting in the way I interacted with individuals, the parables I shared, and the sacrifices I made. Understanding love in its multifaceted nature is essential for those who seek to carry this message into the future.

To begin with, the concept of 'agape' love stands paramount. This is the selfless, unconditional love that seeks the well-being of others without expecting anything in return. It is the love that transcends circumstances, the love that even embraces enemies. In my teachings, I often emphasized the importance of loving one's neighbor as oneself, a command that challenges individuals to look beyond personal interests and to act with kindness, compassion, and generosity. Agape love calls for a radical reorientation of the heart, prompting us to see the divine in everyone we encounter.

In contrast, 'philia' represents the affectionate bond of friendship and camaraderie. This dimension of love celebrates the connections we form with one another—those who share our joys, our struggles, and our lives. I cherished my relationships with my disciples, fostering a community built on mutual support and shared purpose. Philia reminds us of the importance of companionship, encouraging us to nurture our friendships and to extend our love to those within our circles. It is a love that celebrates shared experiences and creates a sense of belonging.

Lastly, there is 'eros', often associated with romantic love. While my teachings primarily focused on agape and philia, eros has its place within the broader tapestry of love. It encompasses the beauty of human attraction and connection, serving as a reminder of the depth and richness of relationships. However, it is essential to approach eros with wisdom and responsibility, ensuring that it is grounded in respect and care for one another.

As I reflect on these dimensions of love, I recognize their interconnection. Agape is the foundation upon which philia and eros can flourish. Without the selfless love of agape, the bonds of friendship and romantic relationships risk becoming transactional or superficial. Love, in its fullness, invites individuals to engage deeply with one another, transcending mere affection to foster profound connections.

In a world often overshadowed by division, misunderstanding, and strife, I hope that future generations will embrace love as a guiding principle. Love has the power to heal wounds, bridge divides, and inspire acts of courage and compassion. It calls for a willingness to see beyond differences and to extend kindness to all, regardless of background or belief.

As you contemplate the message of love, consider its transformative potential in your own life and in the lives of those around you. It is not merely a feeling but a call to action—an invitation to embody the very principles that can bring about change and foster unity. Love, in its many forms, is the legacy I wish to leave behind, and I pray it will inspire you to cultivate a world rich in compassion and understanding.

As I contemplate the future and the legacy of my teachings, I feel compelled to extend a heartfelt call to action for those who come after me. Love is not merely an abstract concept; it is a lived experience that must be embodied in our daily lives. I encourage future generations to actively cultivate love in every interaction, to let it guide their thoughts, words, and deeds.

To embody love means to practice kindness, to choose compassion over indifference, and to embrace the humanity of others, especially those who may be different from us. It is an invitation to break down barriers—whether they be of race, creed, or ideology—and to reach out with open hearts. When love is the driving force behind our actions, we have the power to transform not only our own lives but the world around us.

Throughout my ministry, I witnessed firsthand the transformative power of love in action. For instance, consider the healing of the leper. In a society that marginalized those deemed unclean, my act of reaching out to touch him—something forbidden—was a radical demonstration of love and acceptance. That moment not only healed his body but also restored his dignity and place within the community. This act illustrates how love can break down societal barriers and usher in healing.

Similarly, the story of the woman caught in adultery highlights the essence of love and forgiveness. Surrounded by a crowd eager to condemn her, I chose to confront the accusers instead. My words—"Let any one of you who is without sin be the first to throw a stone at her"—reveal the call to compassion rather than judgment. In extending forgiveness to her, I emphasized that love

transcends sin and shame, offering a path toward redemption and new beginnings.
Even in moments of betrayal, like when Judas turned against me, love remained my guiding principle. I chose to pray for him, recognizing that understanding and compassion are essential, even in the face of deep hurt. This example serves as a profound reminder that love is not contingent upon being treated well; it flourishes in the willingness to forgive and embrace, even amidst pain.
As you carry this message into your lives, remember that love is an action verb. It requires intentionality and effort. It may manifest in small gestures—a kind word to a stranger, a helping hand to someone in need, or a willingness to listen without judgment. Each act of love has the potential to create ripples of change, fostering a culture of empathy and understanding.
I urge you to be love in a world that often feels devoid of it. Seek out opportunities to uplift those who are downtrodden, to embrace those who feel isolated, and to stand in solidarity with those who suffer. In doing so, you become conduits of love, reflecting the very essence of my teachings.
Let love guide your responses to conflict and division. Choose dialogue over discord, understanding over suspicion. When faced with challenges, remember the power of love to transform anger into compassion, fear into courage, and division into unity. The legacy of love is not just a message; it is a call to action that can change lives and heal communities.
In embracing this call, you honor the teachings that have been passed down and fulfill the purpose of your existence. Together, let us strive to create a world where love reigns supreme, a world that reflects the fullness of humanity and the beauty of connection. In this endeavor, we participate in the ongoing story of love that began long ago and continues to unfold in each act of kindness and grace.
The legacy of love extends far beyond individual acts of kindness; it is a transformative force capable of transcending cultural, social, and personal barriers. As I reflect on the implications of my teachings, I recognize that love has the profound ability to connect people across divides that often seem insurmountable.
At its core, love is universal. It speaks a language that resonates in every heart, regardless of background, nationality, or belief system. When we embrace love as a guiding principle, we begin to see the shared humanity that binds us all.

It invites us to look beyond our differences—whether they be race, religion, or social status—and to acknowledge the intrinsic worth of every individual. In a world often marked by division, love serves as a bridge that fosters connection and mutual respect.

Consider the stories of my interactions with those marginalized by society: the Samaritan woman at the well, the tax collectors, and the outcasts. Each encounter demonstrated that love knows no boundaries. In reaching out to those whom others overlooked or rejected, I illustrated that the essence of love is inclusivity. It encourages us to embrace those who are different from us, to learn from their experiences, and to recognize the richness they bring to our communities.

Love also plays a pivotal role in fostering unity among diverse communities. It is a catalyst for dialogue, understanding, and collaboration. When love is present, fear diminishes, and empathy flourishes. This creates an environment where individuals feel safe to share their stories and perspectives, ultimately enriching the collective experience. In moments of tension or conflict, love becomes the anchor that encourages open communication and the willingness to listen.

Moreover, love challenges us to confront and dismantle systemic injustices that perpetuate division. It compels us to stand up against discrimination, inequality, and oppression. When we embody love, we become advocates for those whose voices have been silenced. This advocacy is not just about addressing individual grievances; it is about working towards a society where everyone can thrive. Love empowers us to seek justice, promote healing, and restore dignity to those who have been marginalized.

In envisioning a future shaped by love, I see a world where collaboration replaces competition, and understanding triumphs over ignorance. Communities united in love become beacons of hope, demonstrating the potential for harmony amid diversity. This vision requires intentional effort, as love must be cultivated and nurtured within our hearts and communities.

As you embrace this legacy of love, remember that it is not a passive endeavor. It calls for active participation—engaging with others, advocating for justice, and practicing empathy in everyday interactions. Each small act of love contributes to a larger tapestry of unity, weaving together the diverse threads of human experience.

In doing so, you honor the message I imparted during my time on earth. You become living examples of the legacy of love, inspiring future generations to continue this vital work. By choosing love as your guiding principle, you participate in the creation of a world that reflects the depth and richness of our shared humanity.

Ultimately, the legacy of love is an invitation to dream big and to act boldly. It challenges you to envision a reality where compassion reigns, where diversity is celebrated, and where every individual is valued. In this journey, remember that love is both a destination and a path—a continuous cycle of giving and receiving that transforms hearts and communities alike. Together, let us carry this legacy forward, illuminating the world with the light of love and unity.

Faith serves as a cornerstone for individuals and communities, offering a guiding principle that shapes our understanding of the world and our place within it. It is a deeply personal journey, yet its effects resonate throughout society, creating bonds that connect people to one another and to something greater than themselves.

At its essence, faith embodies trust and belief in the unseen. It provides a framework through which individuals can navigate the complexities of life, especially in times of uncertainty and struggle. When faced with challenges—be it loss, doubt, or despair—faith acts as a beacon of hope, illuminating paths that might otherwise seem dark. It reassures us that we are not alone in our trials; rather, we are part of a larger narrative that extends beyond our immediate circumstances.

In my ministry, I often emphasized the importance of faith. I witnessed how faith can uplift individuals, allowing them to find strength when they felt weak. Whether through the healing of the sick or the redemption of the lost, each act of faith revealed the transformative power that belief can wield. It fosters resilience, empowering people to rise above their difficulties, knowing that there is purpose even in pain.

Moreover, faith plays a pivotal role in shaping communities. When individuals come together in shared beliefs, they create a sense of belonging that transcends individual differences. This collective faith fosters unity, encouraging collaboration and support among members. In times of crisis, a community grounded in faith can mobilize resources, provide comfort, and inspire hope in ways that mere individual efforts cannot achieve.

Faith also invites us to reflect on the values we hold dear. It challenges us to consider what we stand for and how we wish to engage with the world. In nurturing our faith, we cultivate virtues such as compassion, integrity, and humility. These values not only enhance our personal growth but also ripple outward, influencing our interactions with others and the broader society.

In moments of profound uncertainty, faith becomes a refuge. It offers solace when circumstances feel overwhelming, allowing us to release our fears and embrace a deeper understanding of life's mysteries. Through prayer, contemplation, or community worship, we connect with the divine, drawing strength from that relationship. This connection reassures us that there is a greater plan at work, one that we may not fully understand but can trust nonetheless.

As we contemplate the legacy of faith, it is crucial to recognize its role in fostering hope. Faith ignites a spark of optimism, encouraging us to envision a better future, even when current realities seem bleak. It inspires action, prompting individuals to work toward change, to advocate for justice, and to extend compassion to those in need. This proactive stance, born of faith, transforms passive belief into dynamic engagement with the world.

In cultivating faith, we are called to be stewards of hope. This means sharing our beliefs and experiences with others, inviting them into the journey of faith. It encourages dialogue, learning, and mutual support, creating an environment where questions can be asked, and doubts can be explored without fear of judgment.

Ultimately, the importance of faith lies in its capacity to connect, uplift, and inspire. It is a testament to the resilience of the human spirit and the enduring belief in a higher purpose. As you carry this legacy of faith forward, remember that it is both a personal journey and a communal endeavor. By nurturing your own faith, you contribute to a larger tapestry of belief that can uplift others and illuminate paths of hope for future generations.

Let your faith be a guiding light, inviting others to join in the journey of exploration and understanding. Embrace the transformative power of belief, recognizing that it is in our collective faith that we find the strength to overcome challenges and the courage to extend compassion to all of humanity.

As I consider the legacy of faith, it becomes increasingly clear that faith is not merely a passive belief but a call to action. True faith manifests itself through our deeds, compelling us to engage with the world around us in meaningful and transformative ways. It is essential for future generations to understand that faith without action is incomplete; it is through service and compassion that faith finds its fullest expression.

Encouraging future generations to put their faith into action begins with instilling a sense of responsibility toward others. This involves recognizing that each individual is interconnected and that our actions—big or small—can profoundly impact the lives of those around us. Whether it's through acts of kindness, volunteering, or advocating for justice, embodying faith means stepping out of our comfort zones to serve those in need. It means being willing to offer support, to listen, and to stand in solidarity with those who suffer or are marginalized.

Throughout my ministry, I consistently demonstrated the importance of service. From feeding the hungry to healing the sick, each act was not just an expression of love but a powerful testament to the faith that inspired it. These actions illustrate how faith can drive us to address the pressing needs of our communities and the world at large. When individuals come together to serve, they create a ripple effect of compassion that can inspire others to do the same, fostering a culture of care and empathy.

Moreover, faith in action emphasizes the importance of community. Collective faith is a powerful force that can bring about significant change. When people unite under shared beliefs and values, they can mobilize resources, influence policy, and advocate for social justice. This communal aspect of faith nurtures a sense of belonging and shared purpose, enabling individuals to support one another and work collaboratively toward common goals.

Communities of faith can become incubators for positive change, where ideas are exchanged, and collective action is encouraged. In such environments, individuals feel empowered to step forward, knowing that they are part of something larger than themselves. This sense of community not only strengthens personal faith but also enhances the overall impact of service efforts.

Additionally, putting faith into action requires a commitment to continuous learning and growth. It involves recognizing the ever-evolving nature of society and being willing to adapt our understanding of service to meet current needs. This means engaging with diverse perspectives, listening to those who are often unheard, and seeking to understand the systemic issues that contribute to suffering.

Faith inspires us to act with compassion, but it also urges us to reflect critically on our actions and their effectiveness. By fostering an attitude of humility and a willingness to learn, we can ensure that our service is both impactful and respectful of the dignity of those we seek to help.

As you embrace the legacy of faith, remember that putting faith into action is a lifelong journey. It is about cultivating a spirit of service that is woven into the very fabric of your life. Seek opportunities to engage with your community, and let your actions speak to the values you hold dear. Whether through organized efforts or spontaneous acts of kindness, every step taken in faith is a testament to the love and compassion you wish to share with the world.

Let the call to action resonate through future generations as a vital aspect of faith. Encourage them to embody their beliefs through service, recognizing that faith is a dynamic force that can lead to profound change. Together, as a community united in faith and action, they can create a legacy of compassion that extends far beyond their own lives, transforming hearts and minds in ways that echo through the ages.

As I consider the legacy of faith, it's vital to acknowledge that faith is not a static concept; rather, it is a living, breathing entity that can grow and evolve over time. Just as individuals experience changes in their perspectives and understandings throughout life, so too can faith adapt in response to new challenges, insights, and experiences. This evolution of faith is a natural part of the human journey, reflecting our ongoing quest for truth and understanding.

Faith can deepen as we encounter different life circumstances, whether joyful or painful. Each experience—be it a triumph, a loss, or a moment of profound revelation—has the potential to reshape our understanding of faith. These moments challenge us to confront our beliefs, reevaluate our assumptions, and seek a deeper connection with the divine. As we navigate the complexities of life, we may find that our faith matures, becoming more nuanced and reflective of our lived experiences.

Encouraging future generations to embrace the evolving nature of faith involves fostering a spirit of curiosity and openness. It is essential to view questions and doubts not as threats to belief but as invitations to explore deeper truths. Faith should not be perceived as a rigid framework but rather as a dynamic relationship with God that invites dialogue, inquiry, and growth. By engaging with difficult questions and exploring different perspectives, individuals can cultivate a more robust and resilient faith.

Moreover, this journey of faith is enriched by the wisdom we gain from others. Community plays a crucial role in this process, as shared experiences and diverse insights can illuminate aspects of faith that we may not have considered on our own. Interacting with people from various backgrounds and beliefs can challenge us to expand our understanding and embrace a more comprehensive view of faith.

In times of uncertainty, evolving faith can provide a source of strength and comfort. When faced with challenges that shake our beliefs or bring doubt, it is essential to remember that faith can adapt and grow, allowing us to find hope even in the most trying circumstances. Embracing the idea that faith can evolve encourages resilience, reminding us that it is acceptable to wrestle with our beliefs and seek clarity.

Encouraging the pursuit of understanding and wisdom is integral to the journey of faith. Future generations should be inspired to seek knowledge—whether through scripture, spiritual literature, or conversations with wise mentors. This pursuit of wisdom nurtures a deeper connection with faith, enriching both personal understanding and communal discourse. The quest for knowledge fosters a sense of responsibility to share insights with others, creating a cycle of growth that benefits the entire community.

The evolving nature of faith is a vital aspect of its legacy. As you journey through life, embrace the changes in your beliefs and allow them to shape your understanding of the divine. Seek wisdom, engage with your community, and remain open to the lessons that life presents. Faith is not merely a destination; it is a continuous journey of discovery that invites you to deepen your connection with love, truth, and the profound mystery of existence. By cultivating an evolving faith, you contribute to a legacy that transcends time, fostering compassion and understanding for generations to come.

Compassion is a profound expression of love and faith that transcends mere sympathy or pity. It embodies a deep understanding of the struggles and suffering of others, prompting a genuine desire to alleviate their pain. As I reflect on the significance of compassion, I recognize it as a transformative force that has the potential to heal wounds—both personal and communal.

Compassion allows us to connect with one another on a fundamental level, fostering a sense of belonging and solidarity in our shared humanity.

Understanding compassion begins with recognizing its roots in love. Love is not merely an emotion; it is an active choice to seek the well-being of others, to walk alongside them in their suffering, and to offer support without judgment. Compassion invites us to look beyond ourselves, to see the world through the eyes of those who are hurting, and to respond with kindness and empathy. This process of connecting with others allows us to break down the barriers that often divide us, fostering unity and understanding in a world that can feel fragmented and isolated.

Moreover, compassion has the remarkable ability to heal. It serves as a balm for the wounds we carry—wounds that may stem from loss, trauma, or injustice. When we experience compassion, whether given or received, it can profoundly impact our emotional and spiritual well-being. It reminds us that we are not alone in our struggles; it reinforces our inherent worth as human beings and encourages us to extend that same kindness to others. This cycle of compassion can create ripples of healing that extend far beyond the individual, contributing to the overall well-being of families, communities, and even societies.

To truly embody compassion, future generations must engage in practical expressions of kindness and service. Acts of compassion do not have to be grand or heroic; they can be simple gestures that reflect our willingness to care for one another. Whether it's a warm smile, a listening ear, or a helping hand, these actions hold the power to uplift those around us. Encouraging individuals to take small, consistent steps toward compassion can lead to transformative changes in their communities.

Consider the impact of a community coming together to support those in need. When neighbors band together to provide meals for families facing hardship, volunteer at local shelters, or mentor youth in their area, they create a culture of compassion that resonates throughout the entire community. These acts of kindness, no matter how small, can foster a sense of connectedness and inspire others to engage in similar acts. The beauty of compassion is that it often inspires a ripple effect; one act of kindness begets another, creating a chain reaction of goodwill.

As future generations consider their role in promoting compassion, it is essential to recognize the connection between compassion and social justice.

Compassion is not just about alleviating immediate suffering; it is also about addressing the root causes of injustice and inequality. A compassionate heart compels us to confront the systemic issues that perpetuate suffering and to advocate for the rights of those who are marginalized and oppressed. This commitment to justice is a natural extension of a life rooted in love and faith.

Compassion informs our actions against injustice by urging us to stand up for those whose voices are often silenced. It calls us to be allies in the fight for equality, equity, and dignity for all people, regardless of their background or circumstances. This means actively listening to the stories of those affected by injustice, amplifying their voices, and working collaboratively to create systemic change. By advocating for the marginalized, we embody the compassion that is central to my teachings and continue the work of love in the world.

Future generations have the opportunity to cultivate compassion as a cornerstone of their lives, shaping their interactions and decisions in ways that reflect a commitment to justice and equality. This involves recognizing the interconnectedness of humanity and understanding that the well-being of one is tied to the well-being of all. When we embrace this truth, we empower ourselves to effect meaningful change in our communities and beyond.

The call to spread compassion is a vital aspect of the legacy I hope to leave behind. Compassion, as an expression of love and faith, has the power to heal wounds and bridge divides. By encouraging acts of kindness and service, individuals can create ripple effects that uplift their communities and foster a culture of empathy. Moreover, by understanding the role of compassion in the fight for social justice, future generations can become advocates for the marginalized, working to dismantle systems of oppression and promote equality. As you carry this message forward, may you embody compassion in all aspects of your life, fostering a world where love reigns and humanity thrives together in unity.

In reflecting on the barriers that divide humanity—such as race, class, nationality, and ideology—I cannot help but feel the weight of the pain and strife these divisions have caused throughout history. These artificial boundaries often create an "us versus them" mentality, fostering conflict and misunderstanding rather than unity and cooperation. Yet, at the core of my message lies a profound call to transcend these divisions, inviting all people to recognize our shared humanity.

Understanding that we are all created in the image of God is a powerful foundation for promoting unity. Each person, regardless of their background, carries inherent dignity and worth. My teachings emphasize the importance of seeing one another as brothers and sisters, encouraging compassion and empathy in our interactions. By cultivating a mindset that values connection over division, we can begin to dismantle the barriers that separate us. It is crucial to acknowledge that our differences—be they cultural, political, or ideological—should not overshadow our common humanity. Instead, they can enrich our understanding and experiences, providing a tapestry of perspectives that enhance our collective journey.

Imagining a unified future requires a vision where love and compassion guide our interactions. In this world, conflicts are approached with a spirit of dialogue rather than hostility, and understanding takes precedence over judgment. Picture communities where individuals actively seek to understand one another, embracing the beauty of diverse experiences while working collaboratively toward common goals. This vision is not merely an idealistic dream; it is a possibility grounded in the values of love, acceptance, and mutual respect.

Shared values play a pivotal role in bringing people together across differences. When we focus on what unites us—such as the desire for peace, safety, and well-being—we create a foundation upon which to build lasting relationships. These values act as bridges, connecting individuals who may otherwise find themselves at odds. In envisioning a world united by love, it becomes clear that our shared humanity is a powerful motivator for collective action. It inspires us to advocate for justice, to reach out to those in need, and to stand in solidarity with one another.

The power of community cannot be understated in this vision of united humanity. Inclusive communities that embrace diversity are vital in fostering an environment where all voices are heard and valued. When individuals come together with a commitment to mutual respect and understanding, they create spaces where everyone can thrive. This inclusivity allows for the celebration of differences while nurturing a sense of belonging that transcends superficial divisions.

Encouraging future generations to cultivate relationships rooted in respect and understanding is essential in this endeavor. As you engage with one another, remember that each person brings unique experiences and perspectives that enrich the community. Embrace the opportunity to learn from one another, to share stories, and to find common ground. By fostering these connections, you contribute to a culture of compassion that reflects the heart of my teachings.

Moreover, the role of education in promoting this vision cannot be overlooked. Teaching future generations about the importance of unity, empathy, and compassion will equip them to navigate a complex world marked by diversity. Education can serve as a powerful tool for dismantling prejudice and ignorance, fostering understanding among different cultures and communities. When individuals are educated about the experiences and histories of others, they become more likely to empathize and connect on a deeper level.

As I envision this future, I am reminded that it is not merely an aspiration but a calling for each of you. The responsibility to create a more united humanity rests in your hands. Each act of love, each moment of understanding, and each commitment to standing against injustice contributes to the realization of this vision. Your choices matter; they shape the world you inhabit and the legacy you leave behind.

My vision of united humanity is one rooted in love, compassion, and shared values. By transcending the divisions that separate us, we can create a world where understanding and cooperation thrive. Embracing the power of community, fostering relationships based on respect, and educating future generations are essential steps toward achieving this vision. As you carry this message forward, remember that the journey toward unity begins with each of you, and your actions can contribute to a brighter, more compassionate future for all.

As I reflect on the legacy I hope to leave behind, the themes of love, faith, compassion, and unity resonate profoundly as foundational elements that define not only my teachings but also the path forward for future generations. These principles form the bedrock of a life lived in service to one another, encouraging individuals to look beyond themselves and embrace a broader sense of community. Love is not merely a sentiment but a powerful force capable of transforming lives and relationships. Faith provides the anchor that holds us steady during tumultuous times, fostering resilience and hope even in the face of adversity. Compassion is the call to action, urging us to respond to the suffering of others with empathy and kindness. Finally, unity serves as the vision for a world where differences are celebrated, and connections are cherished.

In sharing these reflections, I feel a deep sense of urgency to convey a heartfelt message to those who will come after me. The essence of my teachings is not confined to a single moment in history; it is meant to echo through the ages, inspiring hearts and minds to engage in the work of love and healing. Each generation has the opportunity—and the responsibility—to embody these principles, transforming their communities and ultimately the world. I urge you to carry forward this message with passion and conviction. The world needs individuals who are willing to stand up for what is right, who will advocate for the marginalized, and who will extend compassion to those in need.

The call to be agents of change is not just an invitation; it is a necessity. In a world filled with division, strife, and pain, the need for hope and healing has never been greater. You possess the power to affect change, not only in your own lives but also in the lives of those around you. By embracing love, nurturing your faith, and practicing compassion, you can create ripple effects that extend far beyond your immediate surroundings. Remember that even the smallest acts of kindness can have profound impacts, transforming hearts and fostering a culture of understanding.

I encourage you to take the time to reflect on your role in this journey. How can you contribute to a world that embodies these values? Consider the ways you can spread love in your community—through acts of service, by lending a listening ear, or simply by showing kindness in your daily interactions. Think about how you can deepen your faith, drawing strength and inspiration from it as you navigate life's challenges. Engage with others, striving to understand their perspectives and experiences, and work together to build a more compassionate society.

As you embark on this journey, hold onto the vision of a brighter, united future—a future where love and compassion guide humanity's actions. It is a vision within reach, but it requires dedication and a willingness to act. Your choices matter; they shape the world you inhabit and influence those around you. By choosing love over hate, understanding over ignorance, and unity over division, you pave the way for a more hopeful tomorrow.

Indeed, I affirm the potential that resides within each of you. The legacy of love, faith, compassion, and unity is not just my own; it is a shared heritage that belongs to all of humanity. May you carry this legacy forward with grace and determination, lighting the path for others and inspiring a movement of love that transcends barriers. Together, let us build a world where the essence of these teachings thrives, creating a lasting impact for generations to come.

Epilogue: The Journey Continues

As I depart the physical realm for the final time, I need you to know my spirit is always here. With you.

Remember my journey and teach your children well that my messages echo through time—messages rooted in love, sacrifice, and redemption. Each moment captured in these, my reflections, is not merely a historical account; it serves as a guide, illuminating the path for future generations. In a world often overshadowed by division and despair, these themes stand as pillars of hope and transformation, inviting all to engage deeply with their essence.

Love, at the heart of my ministry, transcends mere emotion; it is a call to action, a transformative force capable of healing wounds and bridging divides. This love is not limited to those who love us in return; rather, it challenges us to extend compassion to all, including those who may oppose or misunderstand us. In an age where misunderstanding often breeds conflict, the imperative to love unconditionally becomes ever more urgent.

Sacrifice, too, is woven intricately into the fabric of this message. It is through sacrifice that we express our deepest values and priorities. The act of laying down one's life for others is the ultimate testament to love's power. Each of us is called to consider what sacrifices we might make in our daily lives to uplift those around us and contribute to a more just and loving world.

Redemption threads through these themes, offering a promise of hope. It reminds us that no matter the depths of despair, there is always a pathway back to grace and renewal. This journey of redemption is not solely personal; it invites us to embrace the possibility of transformation for all humanity.

These interconnected themes of love, sacrifice, and redemption resonate deeply with the human experience. They challenge us to engage with the world around us in a manner that reflects our highest ideals. As we explore these teachings further, may they inspire not only reflection but also action—leading to a life lived in service of something greater than ourselves. This is the legacy I hope to leave: a vibrant call to embody these principles in our everyday lives, nurturing a spirit of compassion that transcends generations.

At the heart of my ministry lies love, an all-encompassing force that transcends boundaries and shapes the very essence of human experience. This love is not merely a sentiment; it is a profound commitment that calls individuals to act with kindness, empathy, and understanding.

Sacrifice is the ultimate expression of love, revealing the depth of one's commitment to others. My life and mission embody this principle, culminating in the ultimate act of sacrifice on the cross. This moment was not merely an event; it represented the profound willingness to lay down one's life for the sake of humanity. Such an act encapsulates the essence of love in its purest form.

The significance of sacrifice extends beyond individual acts; it speaks to the broader narrative of communal well-being. When we embrace sacrifice, we acknowledge the interconnectedness of our lives and the responsibility we hold toward one another. This perspective challenges us to consider what we are willing to give up—be it time, resources, or comfort—in order to uplift others and contribute to the common good.

Embracing sacrifice fosters deeper connections with others. It invites us to step outside of our own needs and desires, creating space for empathy and compassion to flourish. When we choose to sacrifice for the benefit of another, we echo the divine love that calls us to serve, reinforcing the bonds that unite us as a community.

Redemption stands as a central theme in my teachings, embodying the promise of forgiveness and the opportunity for new beginnings. At its core, redemption signifies a transformative journey that allows individuals to rise above their past mistakes and embrace the possibility of renewal. This theme resonates deeply with the human experience, as it speaks to the innate desire for reconciliation and the hope for a better future.

The promise of forgiveness is a cornerstone of redemption. It invites individuals to let go of guilt and shame, extending grace not only to themselves but also to others. In my ministry, I emphasized that forgiveness is not merely a transaction; it is a profound act of love that liberates the soul. When we forgive, we participate in a cycle of healing that restores relationships and fosters a sense of community. This act of releasing burdens enables individuals to move forward with renewed strength, fostering a spirit of resilience that is vital for personal growth.

Redemption is intricately linked to the notion of new beginnings. It reassures humanity that no one is beyond hope, regardless of the choices they have made. The stories of transformation—from the repentant sinner to the prodigal son—serve as powerful reminders that every individual has the capacity for change. Each new day offers a fresh start, an opportunity to align with the values of love, compassion, and integrity. This message resonates across cultures and generations, offering a universal truth that transcends time.

As we contemplate the implications of redemption, it becomes evident that it is not confined to personal experiences; it extends to entire communities and societies. When groups embrace the principles of forgiveness and renewal, they cultivate environments where healing can occur, leading to social transformation. This collective commitment to redemption has the potential to dismantle cycles of violence, prejudice, and despair, fostering a world that reflects the ideals of justice and compassion.

The message of redemption is not just a historical narrative; it offers hope for future generations. It inspires individuals to seek understanding and to believe in the possibility of change within themselves and others. In a world often fraught with division and despair, the promise of redemption shines as a beacon of hope, urging humanity to rise above its struggles and embrace a more compassionate existence.

As we reflect on redemption, we are reminded that it is a dynamic process, one that requires ongoing commitment and introspection. It invites us to confront our own shortcomings and to extend grace to those around us. Through the lens of redemption, we find a pathway to healing and unity, reinforcing the idea that love, sacrifice, and forgiveness are not just ideals to aspire to but essential components of the human journey.

In this way, the theme of redemption embodies a hopeful vision for humanity, inviting each person to participate in a story that is greater than themselves. It calls upon future generations to carry forward this message, embracing the transformative power of forgiveness and the promise of new beginnings, as they work toward a more compassionate and just world.

The themes of love, sacrifice, and redemption are intricately woven together, forming a tapestry that illustrates the essence of my teachings. Each theme complements and enhances the others, creating a holistic understanding of the human experience. Reflecting on this interplay reveals profound insights into how these elements can shape individual lives and society as a whole.

At the heart of my message is love, the foundational principle that underpins all relationships. Love is not merely an emotion; it is an active choice that compels individuals to put the needs of others before their own. This selfless love inspires acts of sacrifice, where individuals willingly give of themselves—be it time, resources, or even their own comfort—for the sake of others. This sacrifice is not only an expression of love but also a testament to the strength of character that emerges when one prioritizes the well-being of the community.

As sacrifice unfolds in the context of love, it paves the way for redemption. When individuals experience genuine acts of love and sacrifice, they often find themselves transformed. Redemption becomes possible when hearts are open to forgiveness and healing. It is through acts of love—whether shown through kindness, support, or understanding—that people are encouraged to seek renewal and embrace the chance to start anew. This cycle illustrates how love begets sacrifice, which in turn fosters an environment where redemption can flourish.

Living out these themes in daily life has the potential to create a ripple effect throughout society. When individuals embody love, their actions inspire those around them, creating a culture of compassion and support. A simple act of kindness can resonate far beyond its immediate context, encouraging others to respond in kind. This interconnectedness highlights the profound impact of living authentically in alignment with these values.

When acts of sacrifice are made with love at their core, they not only benefit the immediate recipient but also reinforce the fabric of the community. Sacrifice invites others to engage in collective efforts, fostering unity and collaboration. Communities built on the principles of love and sacrifice become resilient in the face of challenges, cultivating environments where redemption is not just possible but celebrated.

As these themes intertwine, they also challenge individuals to confront the complexities of life. The journey of love often requires sacrifice, and the path to redemption can be fraught with difficulties. However, it is precisely in navigating these challenges that individuals discover their strength and capacity for growth. The interplay of love, sacrifice, and redemption ultimately cultivates a deeper understanding of what it means to be human—acknowledging imperfections while striving for greater connection and understanding.

In reflecting on the societal implications of these themes, it becomes clear that they are essential in addressing issues such as injustice, division, and despair. Love, as a guiding principle, encourages individuals to advocate for one another, creating movements rooted in compassion. Sacrificial actions, whether large or small, contribute to social change, challenging norms that perpetuate inequality. Redemption offers hope to those who feel marginalized or lost, reminding them that they are deserving of love and new beginnings.

As future generations engage with these intertwined themes, they are invited to create a legacy that embodies love, sacrifice, and redemption. The impact of living out these principles can lead to transformative change, fostering a world where compassion reigns, understanding prevails, and humanity thrives. In this way, the interplay of these themes not only shapes individual lives but also has the power to inspire a collective movement toward a more loving and united world.

Faith is an intrinsic part of the human experience, providing a source of strength and resilience in challenging times. It serves as a guiding light, helping individuals navigate life's uncertainties and instilling hope when circumstances seem bleak. Faith, in its many forms, has the power to inspire acts of kindness and generosity, reminding individuals that they are part of something greater than themselves.

Reflecting on my own journey, it becomes clear how faith has played a pivotal role in nurturing hope. It fosters a sense of belonging, providing comfort in times of sorrow and encouragement during trials. Whether through prayer, meditation, or communal worship, faith nurtures a deeper connection to the divine and to one another. This connection can manifest in acts of service, where individuals extend themselves to help those in need, embodying the very essence of compassion.

Throughout history, many have turned to faith as a source of strength during difficult times. Consider the resilience displayed by those who have faced natural disasters, personal tragedies, or systemic injustices. Faith often acts as a foundation upon which individuals rebuild their lives, igniting a sense of purpose that propels them forward. In these moments, the strength drawn from faith not only uplifts the individual but also inspires those around them, creating a ripple effect of hope and kindness.

Compassion, as an extension of love, plays a crucial role in creating a more humane world. It is the embodiment of empathy and understanding, prompting individuals to take action on behalf of others. Compassion compels us to see beyond ourselves and recognize the shared struggles of humanity, driving us to respond with kindness and support.

As we reflect on these themes, it becomes evident that the teachings of love, faith, and compassion offer a blueprint for future generations. They serve as a guide for living a life that not only benefits oneself but also uplifts others. It is a call to action, encouraging individuals to embody these principles in their daily interactions and choices.

In a world that often feels divided and chaotic, these teachings remind us of the power of unity and understanding. They invite us to cultivate relationships rooted in respect, to listen to differing perspectives, and to engage in acts of kindness that reflect the essence of love. By drawing inspiration from these themes, future generations can contribute to a more loving and compassionate world.

As individuals embrace the teachings of love, faith, and compassion, they become spiritual agents of the Divine. Each act of kindness, no matter how small, has the potential to create a ripple effect, inspiring others to follow suit. By embodying these values, individuals can foster an environment where love flourishes, compassion reigns, and faith guides.

The enduring impact of love, the strength found in faith, and the legacy of compassion are gifts to be embraced and shared. As future generations engage with these principles, they are invited to carry forward the essence of my teachings, transforming the world into a place where love and compassion illuminate the path for all. The call to live these values is not just a personal journey; it is a collective endeavor that holds the promise of a brighter, more united future.

As we reflect on the profound teachings of love, sacrifice, and redemption, it is essential to move beyond contemplation and into action. I encourage you to actively embody these principles in your daily life. Love is not merely an abstract concept; it is a call to engage with others, to uplift and support those around you. Begin by cultivating love in your immediate circles—family, friends, colleagues. Simple acts of kindness, genuine listening, and expressing gratitude can create a ripple effect, transforming relationships and fostering a sense of community.

Consider integrating these themes into your daily actions. For example, in your workplace, strive to create an environment where everyone feels valued and respected. This can be achieved through collaborative projects, inclusive decision-making, and recognizing the contributions of all team members. In your social interactions, practice empathy; seek to understand the perspectives of others, especially those who may differ from you. By doing so, you help cultivate a culture of compassion that prioritizes connection over division.

It is crucial to recognize that you have the power to be a spiritual agent of the Divine in your community. Each one of you possesses unique gifts and talents that can contribute to the collective good. Reflect on the potential for collective action. When individuals unite around a common cause, they can create transformative change that extends far beyond their immediate circumstances.

The legacy of love, sacrifice, and redemption hinges on our willingness to act. Each step taken in the name of compassion not only benefits those directly involved but also inspires others to reflect on their own potential for positive change. Imagine a community where love is the guiding principle, where individuals actively support one another, and where collective action leads to significant progress. You have the power to turn this vision into reality.

Envisioning a world rooted in love, sacrifice, and redemption requires both hope and action. Picture a society where understanding and compassion replace hostility and indifference. Imagine schools that teach empathy alongside academics, workplaces that prioritize well-being and collaboration, and neighborhoods where diversity is celebrated and embraced. This vision is attainable, but it requires dedication and commitment from each of you.

To work toward this future, foster relationships that embody these values. Build bridges between communities and engage in dialogue that promotes understanding. Celebrate differences while seeking common ground. Each interaction offers an opportunity to plant the seeds of love and compassion, nurturing a future where these principles are central to human interaction.

As you reflect on your role in this journey, remember that each of you has the ability to make a difference. Your actions, however small, contribute to a larger movement toward love and compassion. Embrace the call to be a beacon of hope in a world that sometimes feels shrouded in darkness.

Know that the principles of love, sacrifice, and redemption are not just teachings; they are living truths waiting to be expressed through your actions. Let these values inspire you to take bold steps forward, knowing that you are part of a greater narrative of change.

I urge you to carry this message into your lives, to embody it in your interactions, and to share it with others. Together, we can create a future grounded in the enduring impact of love and faith, transforming our communities and, ultimately, the world. Embrace the purpose that comes from living out these teachings, and let them guide you as you strive to make a difference, one act of kindness at a time.

Does my message seem repetitive to you?

Good. I hope so.

My message is a meditation. A meditation that is vital to revisit again and again. The message of love, sacrifice, and redemption stands at the core of our shared humanity. Love, as the most profound and transformative force, has the power to heal, connect, and uplift. Sacrifice, the ultimate expression of love, invites us to look beyond ourselves and serve others, forging deeper bonds within our communities. Redemption offers hope—a promise that no matter the struggles or mistakes we encounter, there is always a path to forgiveness and renewal.

Carrying these teachings forward is essential for shaping a better world. Each of us has the ability to embody love in our actions, to sacrifice for the greater good, and to extend grace to ourselves and others. The importance of these principles cannot be overstated; they serve as a guide for how we navigate the complexities of life and interact with those around us.

As we reflect on the enduring relevance of love, sacrifice, and redemption, let us recognize their potential to inspire change. These themes are not bound by time or circumstance; they are as applicable today as they were in the past. In a world often marked by division and strife, the call to love and serve one another is more urgent than ever. It is through these acts of compassion and understanding that we can collectively strive toward a more harmonious existence.

As you embark on your own journeys, hold onto this heartfelt message of hope and encouragement. You are empowered to make a difference, however small it may seem. Each act of love, each moment of sacrifice, and each opportunity for redemption adds to a collective impact that can transform lives and communities.

I invite you to be bearers of love and light, spreading kindness in your daily interactions. Embrace the potential for positive change within yourself and those around you. Remember that the legacy of love, sacrifice, and redemption is not just a story of the past but a living, breathing force that continues to shape our world. Let your actions reflect these teachings, creating a ripple effect that inspires others to join in this noble pursuit.

In your hands lies the ability to contribute to a brighter future, one that embodies the essence of these teachings. As you move forward, may you be guided by love, driven by compassion, and anchored in the hope of redemption. Together, let us forge a path toward a world where these values reign supreme, ensuring that the legacy we leave behind is one of light, love, and unity.

About Alex Telman

Alex Telman is a globally recognized spiritual healer, author, and one of the country's most read poets. With over 45 years of experience, he has dedicated his life to helping individuals break free from negative energies, trauma, and spiritual blockages. His transformative work has empowered a diverse range of clients, including celebrities, business leaders, educators, and everyday individuals, guiding them toward emotional well-being, personal growth, and spiritual fulfillment.

From an early age, Alex demonstrated extraordinary abilities to perceive and remove harmful energies and entities, a gift that first emerged when he was just three years old. This rare talent led him to study with psychic masters across the globe—Afghanistan, France, Sweden, Israel, England, and Australia—each recognizing his unique gifts and helping him refine his craft.

In addition to his healing practice, Alex has practiced as a barrister, teacher, university lecturer, and small business owner, offering a well-rounded perspective on healing that combines spirituality with practical action. He is also an accomplished author, whose writings inspire and uplift readers by exploring the depths of human emotion and the power of self-healing.

Through his sessions, Alex has helped countless individuals overcome emotional turmoil and reclaim their lives. His work transcends cultural and geographical boundaries, offering profound healing to those in need. His mission is simple yet powerful: to guide people back to their authentic selves, helping them live with purpose, peace, and fulfillment.

With a career built on compassion, wisdom, and deep spiritual insight, Alex remains a beacon of hope for anyone seeking to overcome their struggles and wanting to step into a life of clarity and joy.

Other Titles by Alex Telman

Non Fiction

From Cursed to Cured: 100 True Stories of Healing from Curses
Connecting to the Afterlife: a how-to guide
Your Journey from Death to Rebirth
Empower Your Sundays: Unlocking Inner Strength for a Resilient Life
The Truth Behind the Creation Story: A Journey Through Reincarnation
Practical Mentalism in a Nutshell
Reprogram Your Mind in a Nutshell
Meditation in a Nutshell
Alex Telman in Quotes

Novels

Down and Out in Byron Bay
One Life, Half Lived
Homeless in New York
God Speaks: A Journey Through Creation in His Own Words

Poetry

Echoes of September 11
Burning Echoes of Time
From Dawn to Dusk: the life cycle in sonnets
Eternal Echoes: The Tapestry of Time and the Unseen
Snapshots of People I Have Never Met
Legends and Lessons: 36 Myths Unveiled
A Measure of Time: The Eternal Voyage of Self
Ashes of Verses: Poems Burned But Not Forgotten

Telman: The Complete Haiku 1974-2024
Reflections on Solitude: A Poetic Journey Through The Lonely Mind
Your Friendship is a Museum
Whispers to Bella

Don't miss out!

Visit the website below and you can sign up to receive emails whenever Alex Telman publishes a new book. There's no charge and no obligation.

https://books2read.com/r/B-A-YBSCC-SHXDF

BOOKS 2 READ

Connecting independent readers to independent writers.

www.ingramcontent.com/pod-product-compliance
Lightning Source LLC
LaVergne TN
LVHW050549160826
845677LV00011B/2238